The Joy Journal

For Momma, who loved to journal moments big and small, and whose words are heard long after she has left this earth. Your love for writing lives on in each of your daughters.

**Part One: Her Story**

Story One: Joy through a Good Father

Story Two: Joy After Cancer

Story Three: Joy through Obedience

Story Four: Joy through a Life Miracle

Story Five: Joy through His Plan for My Family

Story Six: Joy through the Valleys

Story Seven: Joy through an Answered Prayer

Story Eight: Joy through Love, Healing and His Goodness

Story Nine: More than I Can Handle

Story Ten: Even When I Feel Alone

Story Eleven: Deep Roots of Faith

Story Twelve: A Touch of Real Love

Story Thirteen: Joy through Healing

Story Fourteen: Bigger than a Diagnosis

Story Fifteen: The Other Side of Addiction

Story Sixteen: Embracing His Plan

Story Seventeen: My God Story

Story Eighteen: Joy through God's Provision

Story Nineteen: I Don't Want to Miss it

Story Twenty: Open Arms

Story Twenty One: "Joy through Infertility"

Story Twenty-Two: Marriage in Crisis

Story Twenty-Three: Community of Support

Story Twenty-Four: Building a Warrior

Story Twenty-Five: The Sun will Come Out

Last December, we were counting down the days until Christmas break, moving around the house on fast-forward, consumed by long to-do lists, last minute homework assignments and wrapping presents for teacher gifts. I had paused to throw a frozen pizza in the oven, when I saw Jonah pass through the living room in his running shorts.

"You headed out?" I asked him, noticing that it would get dark soon.

My son wasn't about to waste a good running day, as temperatures peaked at sixty degrees that afternoon, a rare high in mid- December.

"Yea, I'll be right back," he told me.

He flew out the door and out of my sight as I watched him zig zag away from our house and down the street.

Minutes later I heard the familiar beep of the kitchen stove alerting me that the pizza was ready. With a crowd of littles surrounding me, I began to divvy out the slices one at a time. When I whirled around to deliver the last plate to my two-year old, I caught the flashing screen of an incoming text message on my cell phone.

The words on the screen jumbled in my brain.

"Laura, call me when you get this message. Your son was hit by a car."

My stomach entered my throat as the plate in my hand came crashing to the ground.

I dialed the number so fast I could barely touch the screen. I still hadn't registered what was transpiring.

"Laura, I am calling you to let you know that Jonah has been hit by a car crossing the road on Fairview Drive. We have been trying to get a hold of you. He is okay."

"Josh!" I screamed, interrupting the chaos with desperation.

I gathered the kids to pray as I watched my husband run out the door to head to the scene. The next few minutes were a whirlwind. Questions assaulted my mind as I desperately waited for someone to arrive and take over watching the littles, which included a 3.5 month old.

*Why would I let him go this late?*
*How could I be such a bad mom? This is my fault. I told him to go even though I knew the sun was about to set.*
*Dear God, please let him be okay.*

Moments later, my inlaws arrived, freeing me up to head to the hospital. Driving down the road at a dangerous pace, I saw an incoming call from Josh. A wall of fear rose up within me, warning me not to answer. I accepted the call anyway, taking a deep breath, and pacing myself to hear the very worst. Just last year, we lost my mom in a car accident. This was all too real. The emotions are too raw.

"Laura, Jonah is okay," Josh told me with a steady voice. "They let him get out of the ambulance. He's with me.

When I joined them, Jonah was at the Emergency Room to be checked out from head to toe and rule out internal bleeding. At the welcome counter, we told the receptionist that our son had been hit by a car and she looked around and past us at first looking for someone who had been hit. Finally, we pointed to Jonah and looking skeptical at first, she sent us straight to a room.

Each test that came back said the exact same thing-- they could not find anything wrong with him. While this in itself felt like a miracle, it would be the stories that emerged the next day that truly pointed to the goodness of God in our son's life.

"Call me when you get this," a text message read. We were back home resting from the events the night before.

Hanging up the phone, I could not believe what I heard. The woman who was just ahead of Jonah on the walkway, remembers seeing him out of the corner of her eye. She heard the impact Jonah made with the car and saw him fly through the air. At first she thought it looked like a deer. When it registered with her that a human had been hit, she ran towards the ditch. She heard Jonah repeating the name of Jesus over and over again. When she made eye contact with him, she realized that it was not only a young boy, but our son, and as he crawled up the embankment and out of the ditch, she knew his survival was a miracle.

The women who hit him seconded this story. After striking Jonah with her car, she truly believed for several moments that she had killed someone. Eyewitnesses described his body as "flying through the air," and his launched distance as significant.

But the greatest miracle of all came when we went back to the scene of the accident nearly 24 hours later to look for his phone.

Several groups of people had already been to look. We tried locating the phone using the "find my phone" app and had no luck. Friends and family members had scoured the nearby bushes, tree lines and the roadway. After the final few people attempted to locate the device, I had a bold thought-- "Let's just go and look for your phone, Jonah," I told him.

We had avoided this option at first because after the nerves of the impact had worn off from the night before, Jonah was incredibly sore and very shaken up by all that had transpired. We didn't want to ask him to go back to the place he had been hit.

His only recollection of the accident was realizing that it was getting dark quicker than he had anticipated and turning around to head back to our neighborhood. At the crosswalk he remembers seeing a woman cross the crosswalk in front of him. Out of the corner of one eye, he believed he had plenty of time and from the other direction of traffic, he saw no one. He began to cross at a running pace, and after his body made contact with the vehicle, he remembers it happening so fast that he just hit the water at the bottom of the ditch and began to crawl out. He had no idea how far he had been launched or much more about the accident. He never lost consciousness or experienced any major pain in the moment.

Another account from the scene of the accident said it was as if an angel carried him through the air and allowed him to be set down on the other side of the road. No one who was there that night believed it was possible for his injuries to be so minor- cuts and scrapes instead of internal bleeding or broken bones. When we showed up on the scene to look for Jonah's phone exactly 24 hours later, we never would have guessed that his phone had been launched so far away.

I parked the car on the side of the road as the sun started to dip behind the clouds. I watched Jonah looking up and down the roadway. I noticed the traffic at the crosswalk, with several vehicles plowing straight through instead of even tapping their breaks. I saw my son dig through the brush on the ditch's outer banks. I had so many questions but I was pretty sure he was not ready to answer them.

"Is there where you were crossing, Jonah?" I tried to pry.

"Yes, mom, we already talked about this."

"Where were you actually crossing when you were hit?" I kept digging.

"Mom, I am just trying to find my phone. I have no idea exactly where I was, it was getting dark."

Speaking of getting dark, it was getting darker outside at the moment, too. Fifteen minutes into our scavenger hunt, I said a little prayer that we would recover his phone. It was less about the device itself, and more about closure for Jonah. I dug through some thorny vines to go deeper into the ditch and suddenly I was overcome with gratitude. The water was pretty shallow and the amount of debris and twigs in the area made it hard for me to imagine him crawling up the embankment without greater injury. Staring into the depth of the ditch, I felt a twinge in the pit of my stomach, acknowledging that the scene of the accident was much different tonight, with a healthy and whole son, and nothing missing but an Iphone.

"Mom!" Jonah's voice broke into my thoughts. "Come over here!"

I climbed the shallowest area of the bank to find Jonah standing thirty yards away. In the middle of the field, Jonah was looking down with no major expression on his face.

"It's right here."

Looking down to see his phone perfectly intact, I stood in disbelief. The distance the device travelled demonstrated to me the impact of Jonah and the car. Running with his phone in his hand, he was in the crosswalk just before contact with the front corner of the travelling vehicle. This is an estimation based on the other person in the crosswalk who found Jonah moments later. Picturing his body making contact with a moving vehicle and him not only soaring through the air to land in a ditch, but launching his phone so far away, too, was surreal to me. With the full magnitude of this moment at the front of my mind, I began to say a prayer:

"Lord, don't let us forget the moment where Jonah's life was spared. May this phone be a physical reminder of the goodness of you. Years from now, when he looks back to this day, help him to see your protection over his life."

Being back at the scene of the accident, I was keenly aware of how differently everything could have panned out. When I looked up, Jonah had tears in his eyes. I stood next to him for a long minute to just soak in the goodness of God. Jonah's life had been spared, his phone was found perfectly intact and he was the one who was able to find it.

The real joy came in the days and weeks ahead when anxiety knocked at the door regarding any of our children. I believe the enemy tries to use fear and doubt to get us to question everything, especially after something scary or dangerous happens to someone we love. I would just think back to the moment in that field, when half a dozen people had looked for Jonah's phone, but it was meant for him to find it himself and have a moment of gratitude and closure. This moment, as we encountered the goodness of God, my heart began to search for other testimonies that displayed God's love in the big things and the small moments, too.

    -Laura

Dear Joy Journaler,

First of all, I am so glad you are willing to take this journey! This is not a year-long devotional or a six week program. Instead, this is a move-at-your-own-pace challenge to pause in the moment and record a moment of Joy in your life. I have stacks and stacks of journals that I have started over the years, and it's very rare for me to make it to the end of any of them before picking something else up. It's fun to find them though--whether barely started, outlined with doodles and scriptures, or full to the brim. Some of my journals come from happy times, some hold my secret thoughts during dark moments, and others tell my story from day-to-day life. My hope is that the Joy Journal will be different. One might think of this as their "pause" journal, and you may even re-visit it years later to find little reminders of the goodness of God.

Many of us have faced moments where we question our faith. We live our lives on fast-forward, proclaiming we are full of hope, but when circumstances send us straight to our knees, we realize how quickly that faith can be shaken. On January 3, 2022, my mom was killed in a car accident just a year after we lost two babies. Sometimes when I look back at pictures of myself, I divide them into two different categories-- what I looked like before my wilderness season of grief and loss-- and what I look like now, as I try to navigate the waters of healing. I long to be whole to help others navigate the same circumstances that once blinded me.

    Searching through my mom's things a few days after her funeral, I found dozens of journals she wrote in daily. Reading her entries was like learning about her through a different lens, appreciating her innermost thoughts when I used to interact only with the woman I thought I knew. Like me, she struggled with what people thought of her, eagerly worked to earn the affections of people who did not deserve her, and wrestled with self-doubt. Reading her story through these journals showed me the importance of reflection. I learned to appreciate the times in my mom's day that she stopped to pause. As I learned more about her, I became grateful that her words outlived her physical time here on earth.

    This is not the only time I have encountered the power of journaling. When I first started teaching,the sense of overwhelm was real. I can remember feeling like I was drowning. I put out a lot of different fires every day inside my middle school writing classroom. My mentor bought me a journal as a gift, and I decided to use it as a pausing tool to jot down what went right each day at school. When I read the pages back to myself at the end of the school year, I was grateful for how far I had come and all that I had learned in just two semesters. I kept that journal so I can read about the good days often, even though sixteen years have passed.

What will this journal do for you? Will you WRITE, LIST or DRAW your thoughts? Will you PAUSE when you're feeling grateful, PAUSE when you are overwhelmed and PAUSE at all the times in between when you just need a minute to reflect? When you read your thoughts later, you will be amazed how far you have come! After all, Psalms 30:5 tells us that "weeping may last for the night, but JOY comes in the morning," and I have learned firsthand that the night won't last forever. Recording moments of joy provides a powerful reflection tool.

This journal is broken into two parts-- the first is a collection of testimonies from women who have seen the goodness of God in their lives. This half of the journal is called Her Story. I always get wrecked by people's testimonies and as I was preparing to share a few of them in these opening pages,

I felt like I heard the voice of God speaking: "Why are you telling their stories? Let them tell it themselves."

I began to reach out to women who I knew had a story to tell, women who I look up to, women I honor and respect, women who have authenticity and courage. Each "yes" that came back for this joy journal project represents a "yes" to share breakthroughs that might lead YOU to a breakthrough, too. Knowing the background stories of some of these women created some questions for me as I began to read the words that came in.

"Lord, this woman shared that there was a healing miracle in her life. But my other friend writing her story lost a parent to cancer. Why weren't they healed, too?"

"Lord, this sweet lady prayed for a pregnancy miracle and she gave birth to a perfect child. Another one of my precious friends never saw that same miracle. She is still waiting."

"Lord, you spared my son when he was hit by a car. I have dear friends who have lost their child. How do we make sense of the testimonies of hope, divine intervention, and healing juxtaposed with tragedy, loss and death?"

How do I respond to someone who has been on the devastating side of an unanswered prayer and they question the goodness of God?

When I look at it on the surface, it just doesn't make sense. Some losses are completely unfair. Some life altering events do not seem to carry "good" with them. Where is the goodness of God in the unanswered prayers? I was listening to a worship song the other day and my heart leapt within my chest. I sensed a piece of the answer was emerging. In Firm Foundation by Cody Carnes, he sings:

"… Oh, rain came and wind blew
But my house was built on You
And I'm safe with You
I'm gonna make it through"

In the scripture, Matthew 7:24-29, it says:
24"Therefore everyone who hears these words of mine and puts them into practice is like a wise man who built his house on the rock. 25 The rain came down, the streams rose, and the winds blew and beat against that house; yet it did not fall, because it had its foundation on the rock. 26 But everyone who

hears these words of mine and does not put them into practice is like a foolish man who built his house on sand. 27The rain came down, the streams rose, and the winds blew and beat against that house, and it fell with a great crash."

The truth of the matter is that the rain IS going to come. The wind IS going to blow and the waves are going to beat against the house. The outcome of how one handles trials is less about what happens to each of us and all about our foundation in Him. If Christ truly is my "firm foundation," then even in the darkest times, I carry a hope that won't make sense to those around me. I won't get all the answers earthside, and some things will not make sense, but I don't have to have all the answers to recognize that he can move even in the midst of tragedy.

The second half of this journal is called "My Story." Each day there is a scripture to reflect on and a big blank page so you can create whatever you want to. How beautiful--this journal holds numerous testimonies from women in every walk of life. Their life lessons illustrate the journey of finding joy, so you can be encouraged by the testimony of others and believe God to "do it again." It will carry pieces of your story, too!

# Her Story

## Story One: Joy Found in a Good Father

Fire and brimstone.

When I was a kid, I was scared of God. I never had the image of a three headed monster or a giant hairy beast. The image I had of God was like that of many kids, an old man with white hair. But it wasn't His looks that intimated me as a child. I feared His judgement. Raised Catholic, I was taught that there were mortal sins. There were things that we could do and never be forgiven. Over the course of my childhood, I went to church every Sunday, every Holy Day, every Holiday, and once a month for confession. I went through the motions, never understanding why.

As I got older, and started finding my place in the world, I lost my connection to church. I skipped here and there at first. But, the more I found myself playing around in worldly games, I was scared to return. I was scared of God. I had already sinned so much, what was the point? I knew I didn't deserve forgiveness and I knew I was too far gone. It wasn't until I was 26 years old that I even thought about faith. I had always been taught religion. But never truly about faith. Not until it was the only thing I had. From the age of 26 to 28 I was in spiritual warfare. My dad was dying of cancer, I was pregnant with my second child, in a failing marriage, unhappy at work, drinking regularly, and going through the motions of life. I was a complete facade. On the outside I thought I looked like I had it together. But the truth is I was slowly falling apart.

I lost my dad in September of 2016. It was one of the hardest things I have ever experienced. But before my dad died, he told me something that I would never ever forget. He told me, "Honey, I can do way more for you up there than I ever could down here." And over the course of the next year, I saw him do more. I knew that my earthly father was gone but I realized very quickly that I needed my heavenly one. I stepped foot into church for the first time in over a decade on November 26, 2017. I don't know why but on that particular day, God wrecked me. I was 28 years old and never did understand what it meant to feel the presence of God or to be "saved." But that day. That day something I have never experienced before happened. I fell to my knees and wept. I begged God to help me.

I walked away that day thinking things would be easy now. My marriage would be saved. My finances would fall into place. I just knew it. I just had this feeling that all my problems were going to be fixed. Until they weren't. From that moment on... things got HARD. The spiritual warfare I had experienced had just begun. For the next two years, I experienced pain, loss, shame, and guilt that was greater than anything I had ever before. Satan was after me. God was after me. But I had zero discernment.

I started to run. I hated running almost as much as I hated the war my mind was in. I could barely run a mile when I started. Each day I would run and worship. A mile or two a day. On Sunday, I would add a mile, until I got up to 9 or 10 miles a run. I would run for hours asking God to save me. To help me. To heal me. To forgive me. Then step back into the world and sin. I didn't understand why it was so hard. Why was I unable to just "be good enough" to be a Christian?

One day I was on mile 5 of 9. And God spoke to me. He was so clear in His instructions that I finished my run early and ran home. From that moment on, my life took a brand new direction. With it, came great loss. I lost a marriage of 7 years. I lost friends. I lost comfort. I lost time with my kids. I lost respect. The list goes on.

But what I gained... was faith and a father. I learned so many things during that season of loss. I learned how to rely on God for everything. I learned that the image of God I had as a child wasn't the real image of God. I learned that God is a good father. I learned that He is faithful. That He is forgiving. And that He is loving. I learned that He does discipline us when needed, but that He never forsakes us.

God has always been good in my life. He had saved me numerous times but I didn't notice it. Looking back now I realize that God never left my side. He was just waiting for me to accept His love.

I couldn't imagine my life without God and I hate that I spent so long running from Him because of fear of rejection. Because of shame and guilt. Because the truth is no matter how bad I was… God was always good.

-Andrea

## Story Two: Joy after Cancer

*Dear Heavenly Father,*
*We come to you with thanks and praise. You're a just GOD, you're a Sovereign GOD, the One and Only, the First the Last, the Alpha the Omega, the Great I Am. Use me as a vessel to glorify you. In Jesus' name I pray. AMEN*

    As God's story continues in my life, I have tried to be obedient to share my journey, GOD's story. There are a couple of things I would like for you to know. First, as I initially began preparing to jot down some key notes, what I realized more than anything is that it wasn't even actually my story. This is God's story. So everything you read, please understand it is only being provided to glorify God. I am nothing more than a character in His story.

    CANCER. My cross, my blessing. I was diagnosed with Advanced stage 4 cervical cancer, non-operable, incurable in May 2018. I will never be cancer free because the cancer has travelled. Well, at least that's what the doctors say. Through this journey God has spoken to me and I have learned the difference between God's voice and Satan's voice. Sometimes Satan's voice is just reminding me of the reality of my diagnosis. That's where faith comes in and worry ends.

This story began one Sunday in April 2018 when Jae Sims (our church music minister at the time) told us a story that his sweet mom, Cherry Sims, had been diagnosed with breast cancer. He spoke of her having a win-win attitude regarding her cancer. Either she beats cancer and gets to stay here on earth with her family, children, and grandchildren, or she doesn't beat it and she gets to spend eternity in heaven with Jesus and wait for them. This was so powerful of a message for me that day. The rest of that service, that was all I could think about. And even after church it dominated my thoughts. I talked with Todd, my husband, about this powerful message, and I called my best friend to talk with her about this life-changing attitude. I know that God meant for me to hear that that day, BECAUSE; it seemed no one else picked up on the conversation at all that Jae told the church that day.

Two or three weeks later I developed a pain like no other. So intense. After several trips to the doctors and ER, my pain continued to get worse despite the medications prescribed. During this time God had spoken to me. I had been up for nearly 72 hours. I was crying out to God in exhaustion and pain then I heard God's voice say to me "The doctors will heal you." Instantly, peace came over me and I knew that I had a plan. At that point I laid my cross down at God's feet (truly surrendered it) and picked up trust and belief. From that moment, I had no fears, no worries, no stress, no anxieties. The next day Todd took me to the ER and I was admitted for pain management.

While in the hospital the pain continued and if anything seemed to be getting worse. Now during this time, independent of everything else that was going on, my daughters-in-law were in the midst of designing a t-shirt to support me in this fight with cervical cancer. Todd made the suggestion to add a particular scripture verse to the back of the t-shirt. It was Mark 5:34. "He said to her--Daughter, your faith has healed you. " Go in peace and be free from your suffering."

Then on May 12th, my best friend brought me a daily devotional book. It was pink (my favorite color) and so I was excited to see what it showed on that day. It read "HEALER: Daughter your faith has made you well. Go in peace and be healed of your affliction. Mark 5:34  God was speaking to me again, confirming to me that He truly was going to fulfill His promise.Theres no way those two things are a coincidence.
In the next couple of days, the doctor came in to tell me the severity of the diagnosis. That is the moment I learned initially

of it being Stage 4, non-operable and incurable. At that given moment, my husband Todd was not actually with me. While he had not left my side since the beginning, I had convinced him to go get something to eat with our best friends and daughters. But even before they went into the restaurant he called to check on me and I told him what the doctor had just told me.

    I remember the conversation plainly. He irrationally yelled, "What do you mean incurable!" I said to him: "Well, Todd you know what incurable means."

    He continued to react irrationally. Finally, I said: "Todd, calm down. They don't know what I know." From that moment on, he believed and surrendered just as I had. I can confirm that the peace that has come with that surrender is real and life changing. It truly transcends all understanding.

    For the next several days no significant changes occurred. The doctors continued to up my pain medication yet it still wasn't really under control. I was in the hospital for 8 days-- $50k worth of pharmaceuticals pumped through my body. I share that to show the magnitude of my pain and the majestic outcome. On the 6$^{th}$ day at 7 pm a prayer service rallied and approximately 200 people showed up. Just prior to it starting, my pain was severe, and it took everything I was allotted just to be able to stand at the window. What an amazing sight! Seeing so many people that had taken time to come and pray for me and my family it was very emotional to say the least. So many were part of this church body. For we know God tells us, "whenever two or more are gathered in my name, I am there." I knew HE was there HE was in the hospital with me.

The next morning, day 7, I woke up and the pain was gone! Gone!! I mean zero. I tell you this so that you please get plugged in. The power of your church family and prayer warriors is so important. This was also the same day I would receive my initial dose of chemo. I did so enthusiastically. I told God,"let's do this. I will gladly take this but please spare a baby or child of this dreadful disease." After just my third chemo treatment, I had a scan. The results were that all the tumors in my neck and chest had been resolved and the large tumor in my cervix had been reduced 75%. The radiologist in his report used the word, dramatic response.

Then I had three more chemo treatments. Afterwards, I was scheduled for another scan. Just before receiving the results, I was actually out running some needed errands. That in itself was unusual because of the medicine and fatigue. I was on Hwy 54 at a red light when I saw the blue angels practicing. Then amazingly, at that given moment, they made a perfect cancer ribbon in the sky. Right in front of me. I immediately started to cry tears of joy and searched for my phone to take a picture and call Todd. I knew that was God speaking to me again through the Blue Angels this time. I knew the results of the scan were going to be good. And sure enough a couple of days later I received a call from the doctor's office. All of my tumors were resolved. My oncologist made the statement that I had had the best response to chemo in his 27 years of practice. GOD had stayed true to His promise to me that the doctors would heal me.

During this journey God has shown me how we are to love each other. I have been blessed with a love of people. But now that love is stronger. The other thing I noticed was that when we would be out, which wasn't much, the treatment that I would receive was kind because you could visibly see I had cancer. It was very touching. But that's where I also think we fall short. I don't think GOD intended us to only do it to those who we can see their cross. How much better would this world be if we loved each person we encountered everyday as if they had a life threatening cross they were carrying.

I continued to receive maintenance chemo for approximately six years but recently have stopped those treatments altogether. So now, nearly 7 years removed from my initial diagnosis, I proudly as a Daughter of the King of Kings, want to encourage you in your journey. He is a loving and faithful Father. You simply must seek Him with all of your heart. That is His only desire.

Certainly, I will NEVER FORGET the miracle that God has done for our family. And just one more thing before I close. It is important that you know that I'm not special. We are all made in His image. So the same God that healed my incurable cancer, which is my cross, can also heal whatever cross you may have!!!

-Tammy

## Story Three: Joy through Obedience

When I received a text from Laura asking me to share a testimony, the Lord quickly reminded me about the journey He had my husband and I on when we moved away to Florida and then back to Kentucky.

Ministry in Owensboro had left me hurt and disappointed, and I just wanted to escape and never return. It was my hope that our next adventure would wipe away the painful memories. Little did I know, He would bring me back to the pain and restore my heart and the hope of my calling.

I remember Steve, my husband, being hesitant about the move out of Kentucky. He told me that if our house sold quickly and I got a job, it would be confirmation that we should move to Florida. Steve was able to transfer with his job, but we didn't want to move ahead of God. As the Lord would have it, our house sold in less than 24 hours and I was offered four different teaching jobs that I could choose from.

After moving to Florida and accepting a teaching job, I would then step into one of the most pivotal moments in our marriage that I'll never forget. It was July of 2019. I was preparing to send Olivia, our two year old, to daycare and I had so many things to get ready for my new classroom. I just could not move forward. There was this incredibly deep, uneasy feeling I had that I just could not shake. I felt like the Lord was inviting me into a season of rest and I felt Him asking me to quit my job.

How could I share this news with my husband when we were banking on my insurance and income to sustain us in our new move?

Tears streaming down my face with nervousness, I approached Steve with one of the hardest conversations. It was beautiful in the way that he met me with such grace. He agreed with me and then began to share that he felt he was to do the same. Naturally, we looked crazy moving 920 miles across the country to quit our jobs. It was a year of healing and trusting the Lord for both of us.

Looking back at my journals, where I would pour my heart out to the Lord, I came across an entry on August 23, 2019: "The other day when I was driving in Bonita Springs by these big new houses, the Lord began to talk to me and tell me to start believing Him for something bigger." He took me to the scripture in Isaiah 62:4 that says, "Your land will be like a wedding celebration."

Right before COVID hit, Steve came out of the bedroom and told me that the Lord had spoken to him about some family property and that he felt we were to ask his dad for the land and move back to Owensboro. It would be a place called The Refuge, where we would host people and give them a place of rest. I didn't want to return to the painful place I left, but I trusted Steve and that he heard from the Lord. That next week, we drove 16 hours to Owensboro and received 13 acres of land. I was in awe of God's promise to me: "your land will be like a wedding celebration."

That same week while in Owensboro, our friends told us of a house in their neighborhood that was for sale. It was double the price we wanted to spend or even could afford for a home. I remember walking into the front door and hearing the Lord say, "Because of your obedience, I am stretching your tent pegs and giving you this gift of a home." We had tried with multiple banks to get a loan to buy a home in Florida and we were denied every time. We both were jobless and had no idea how the Lord would come through for us BUT God did!

The first bank in Owensboro gave us the loan and the Lord blessed us with what I asked Him for back in 2019.

Isn't it beautiful how the Lord works? It's like He knew there was something greater for me but before I got there, I had to walk through some walls. Even now, I still continue walking through walls, but it gets easier with time and trust with the Lord. And the painful memories are now opportunities for me to be grateful of Him walking with me through it all.

These last three years of being in ministry have been some of the hardest, most rewarding years of me learning how to trust Him and invite Him into areas of my heart that I never knew existed. And to think I have the honor to walk alongside people in their journey with Him. Why me Lord? I hear Him gently whisper, "Because you are obedient to follow me and live a life of faith".

-Faith

## Story Four: Joy through a Life Miracle
(Shared through the Point of View of my granddaughter Emma)

"Trust in the Lord with all your heart, lean not to your own understanding" or that of others, even the professionals. Prov. 3: 5-6 God has plans!!

Grandbaby #5's own LIFE MIRACLE story, as told by Emma Rose.

Extreme pain in the abdomen, better get Mommy to the hospital and see what's wrong, but "check things out first, I might be pregnant" with Kaleb's new baby brother or sister. The ER room says, nope not pregnant so we'll run all the tests, X-rays and stuff to see where the pain is coming from...Can't find anything.... sent Mommy home.

WHAT!!! OH GOD!!! Two weeks later, Mommy was pregnant with me! I'm Mawmaw's first granddaughter! I have to be OK!! Don't say all those things about what's going to be wrong with me since they did all those tests. Don't say the chromosomes are messed up. Don't say I won't live but a few months with Mommy! I want to live! I have to live! Doctors tell Mommy to go home and if I'm still alive in 4 months then they are going to explain to them what all will be wrong with me.... I say NOTHING!! I will live and not die! I will declare the miracles of God.

You see, my name is Emma, which means Healer. I will be born the same year that Prophet Bob Jones says that God has released the Angel Emma and that there will be miracles and healing all over the world to increase. Watch me grow and live!

And that my family did. Every month they'd check Mommy out and report to her things that had to be prayed through. The Holy Spirit even gave Mawmaw and my 3-year-old brother Kaleb a song to sing the whole time I was being made.

"Emma Rose, Emma Rose, you are healed from your head to your toes. Emma Rose, Emma Rose, everything grows the way God says it grows.

Emma Rose, Emma Rose we listen to God and not the enemy's woes." I heard that song so much but it helped me to keep growing. It was funny how every time they sang that song Kaleb would say, " Mawmaw, what is enemy woes? I don't like that."

One day while playing in the playroom Holy Spirit told Kaleb to go tell Daddy something. He told Mawmaw, "God says go tell Daddy…"

"Go tell Daddy what, Kaleb?"

God says, "Tell Daddy, don't worry Daddy, don't worry."

Mawmaw took Kaleb by the hand downstairs to Daddy and Kaleb told him. Then Mawmaw was a bit worried because Daddy doesn't get upset easily. She knew that the doctor's visit today was going to give a bad report. And he did, but we're still believing for me to be strong and healthy. I'm about 6 months in Mommy's womb now and they say some things are not right, like the umbilical cord isn't even made right. They also see something in my lungs. Then they go and tell Mommy that if I live to birth that I might even die when she delivers me. Man, who's telling all this stuff...I feel fine!! God has plans for me...

Pray, pray, pray for the next few months until it's time for me to make my grand entrance. Ok guys, this has got to be good. MY debut, proving to everyone that I'm OK...

Mommy tells daddy, "It's time!" Daddy gets to the hospital and drops Mommy off at ER to go park the car. When

Daddy comes into the ER they don't let him in because he had a pocket knife on his key ring.... He has to fill out forms and they are calling him on the loudspeaker to come now! Well, the guard won't let him leave. After a while they take daddy to the labor department only to find out that Mommy didn't make it to the labor department. I'm coming now!! Mommy is by herself out in the hallway remembering what the doctor said about how I could possibly die at birth. But Mommy finds out that God is all she needs and everything will be OK. But where is Daddy? Ready or not....Here I come!!!

Daddy makes it to the room after I'm already here.... he just puts his head on Mommy and cries...they both cry.... Hey guys.... I'm here and I'm PERFECT!! The most beautiful dark haired little girl in the world. So much for Mawmaw on her way to video my entrance...I didn't wait for her....

So, I'm sure you're asking, "What about the spot they saw in my lungs?" Well remember that chromosomal mess up that they talked about? It all landed in my lungs. A mass of tissue just sitting there....SO when I'm 6 months old they go in and take it out. Daddy and Mawmaw go to give blood in case I need it...you know, you gotta keep it all in the family. But when they gave the blood for it to be used during my surgery, the blood bank ruined it.... So much for that!!

However, as it turns out, God knew I wasn't going to need it anyway. I was supposed to be in the ICU for a few days and then a regular room for a few more days. Who has time to waste in this place? I'm breaking out.... The nurses weren't too happy with me crawling all over the place only a few hours after surgery. They said, "This baby doesn't need to be in the ICU." I think they just didn't want to have to keep up with me. I was in and out of the hospital for about 3 days and back home. Yes, I'm on my way to being a healer for the Lord's glory.... I'm going to live up to my name. Praise God for His faithfulness, to Jesus for healing and to the Holy Spirit for giving all my family the guidance of how to pray in faith and believe for God's best.

Never give up and never agree with the negative reports...God has a plan and He will see them.

-Gaye

## Story Five: Joy through His Plan for My Family

Throughout my life, I have experienced some amazing moments with the Lord. Like remarkable, intimate, life changing, never wanting to end encounters with Him. I have also experienced trials and conflicts that played significant roles in where I am today. All while projecting me closer to Jesus and learning to trust Him more. Let me start at the beginning and hope that I don't lose you in all of it. So, stay with me.

Growing up, I had a Dad who loved Jesus immensely and taught me the things of the Lord at an early age. I was in Church, tent revivals and even at women's prisons while watching my Dad help minister as often as I could. I feel like that played a role in why I was born again at such a young age of 7. I remember that being my first real life, personal encounter with Jesus himself. I had a lot of growing to do, but I knew the things of the Lord and was excited to grow in them.

When I was a teenager, my desire/ lifelong goal or really, "What are your plans after high school" type thing became simple. I wanted to be a Wife and Mom! When I was young, all I wanted to play with was baby dolls. I remember being a preteen and my Grandma asked me would I rather have money or a new doll and can you believe I said doll?!?!

Skip forward to high school and everyone has their own big plan after graduation. Be a nurse, go into cosmetology or be a veterinarian. Me?? I just wanted to be married and have babies.

Great ambition, as pure and honorable as it could be, quickly became a thought of, "how can I make this actually happen on my own?!" So, after an amazing first year or so in high school, of talking about Jesus, bringing friends to Church with me. Seeing them be saved and baptized, walking out the "go ye into all the nations" .... my junior and senior year literally became a fight to survive. Not physically, but spiritually.

I had a football player fall for me. We dated and moved very quickly. He proposed and I said, "yes!" Bought the dress and everything! But let me tell ya a little behind the scenes... I loved Jesus but I began to let my guard down -to be admired and pursued. Seasoned church people would say, "I opened the door for the enemy." When he proposed, all I could think about is how I was going to get to be a wife and Mom. The -sinful- thought was, "I'm engaged now and going to spend my life with him, so why not give him all of me?!" The downward spiral begins here.

    Day after day we would sneak and lie in order to have inappropriate intimate time. You adults know what I mean. Anything outside of Gods' real bounds of marriage is SIN! Time after time, over and over and then I would cry privately after because of how convicted I was. I was living wrong and knew it but couldn't stop. Guess I should admit, I wouldn't stop. It went so far wanting to become a Mom so young and he didn't, so he bought me the "day after" pill. I pretended to take it all while hiding it, then tossing it out a window. THANKFULLY I never became pregnant. This is a big part of the story you see. I wanted something so bad, but it wasn't the right time or person. The GOODNESS of God showed me unbelievable mercy. I eventually gave in to my convictions, he broke off the engagement and I broke up with him for good my senior year.

    You would think everything stopped there. Physically it did, but there was so much healing that needed to take place in me daily to walk the right road moving forward. Lots of repentance took place. Not just between me and Jesus, but the people I hurt too, like my parents.

That was a hard part of my life to talk about. I wish it never happened. I still feel shame trying to creep up every now and then, but I remind myself, it's under the blood of Jesus and He remembers it no more. (Psalms 103:12) After this part of my life was over, I still desperately wanted to be a Wife and Mom. But I matured and knew in God's timing, it would happen and not my own. This season that came next in my life, was a gift straight from my loving Father and it was named Karl.

For months I would read my Bible and write down things on a piece of paper that I wanted my forever mate to have. I think when it was completed, I had like 53 things listed. A couple of my close friends can verify this, I was a bit particular moving forward you could say.

I had a Family friend invite me to a worship rally that was taking place at a Church in Owensboro. (this church happened to be Laura Murphy's Church at the time) Before service started, I saw this guy wearing all black from head to toe pacing the altar, back and forth praying. Then during service, he joins a ministry team up front, and he begins to dance. I heard the Holy Spirit, clear as day tell me, "THAT IS YOUR HUSBAND."

I know, I know... some of you reading this probably are rolling your eyes. But I promise you, this is one of the clearest moments I have ever heard something from Heaven.

I didn't know the person sitting to my right, but I leaned in to her and said, "I don't know that guy's name, but I'm going to marry him one day." I even came home that night and told my Parents, I had met my future Husband. They were like, yea right Ashley. But they are my witnesses to all this. Crazy enough, we were dating a few months later, engaged, then married 6 months after that. ***September 2006 God gave me the gift I was waiting for. My Husband, Karl.

See how God took something that was so broken and bad and replaced it with His perfectness and all his goodness?! HE was long-suffering and forgiving when I needed him most. And now HE was a gift giving Father that showed me so much love and gentleness.

Well, here we were living a cute simple married life and I was ready to be a Momma! Karl knew that before we were married. He didn't want kids so soon like I did, but I was ready to make 'em on the honeymoon!!!

I was having lots of pain in my lower pelvic area for a long time, went to the hospital for exploratory surgery and found HUGE ovarian cysts. The only way to make them go away was shots that could throw me into early menopause or getting pregnant. Weird options huh? Well, my decision was made for me at a later time, after coming home from vacation...I took a test and WAS PREGNANT!!! That very, very faint line was everything to me. I WAS GOING TO BE A MOM!! Throughout my pregnancy, I gained an immense amount of weight and had multiple ultrasounds because of something wrong with my placenta. But being able to see my baby each time and that small beating heart was worth it. February 28th 2008, God gave me a Son, Elijah and granted me the desire of my heart to become a Mother.

Then, less than a year later, gave me my Daughter Honour. It was so hard at first. We were newly married, so young, just bought our first home and honestly, didn't know what we were doing. But the Lord helped us along the way. Remember- I wanted to be a Mother so bad, all my life and God gave me my children when HE saw fit. He breathed life into them, when it was their appointed time- not mine. All my dreams had come true. Ahhh, the goodness of God.

Skip forward sixteen years to 2024......

My old Church was having a guest speaker Todd Smith. His ministry was focused on something called, Fire on the water. I thought it would be amazing so of course my kids and I attended. God moved and I remember saying if he comes back again, I'll get in the water. Well, in September, he was coming back again to minister. They were doing what he calls, "immersions." It had nothing to do with Todd himself, only him walking in obedience to the Lord , in order to see a move of God and people healed and delivered. You see, I wanted to meet Jesus in the water. I wanted a fresh encounter with Him. I walked in, sat down in the warm water and kept my eyes closed. Someone asked, "what are you wanting from the Lord?" I responded with two things. 1) My heart to physically be healed and to come off my heart medicine that I have been on for three years.  2) revival in my Family.

"Are you ready?" He asked as I prepared to be immersed.

I went under, came up and sat still for a few minutes trying to soak it all in.

Then, I heard "I feel like I need to dunk you again."

This time when I came out of the water, I felt different. I gasped for air and felt like I was weightless. Before I even walked out of the baptism waters, I knew everything was different. I got dressed, walked down to my Family and proclaimed, "I feel so different!"

I want you to know, my heart diagnosis was mitral valve prolapse with regurgitation and tachycardia. I would have severe palpitations that would bring me to my knees and make me lose my breath over and over daily. So I was put on once daily medicine for years. And as far as my family was concerned, we loved Jesus- but we weren't putting him first like He should be, whatsoever. I knew I wanted revival in my home.

Since coming out of the water, I have been off my heart medication completely!!! Praise the Lord, He healed my body!

Since that time the enemy hasn't laid low. Why would he? God's Word says that Satan's mission is to steal, kill and destroy and over the last few months, that is exactly what he has tried to do. We had hit after hit, things in our home would break, like our water line bursting- God sent friends that would help dig and big equipment at just the right time.

He also became our provision when we needed miracles. I experienced heartbreak in relationships with friends that I thought would last forever. I would feel bitterness and rage creep up, but God reminded me of His love and forgiveness to me- so I had to let things go and move forward. We battled health scares and many other things, but one last big thing that happened was with our son Elijah in November.

I was eating in town with Honour and my Sister and got a phone call from my Husband Karl. He told me Elijah was just in a wreck and I should probably come out there. So thinking it was something small, because there was no panic in Karl's voice, I got up and headed that way. Only to get another phone call five minutes later, telling me to go to the hospital, the ambulance was taking him. I asked, "why is the ambulance taking him???"

What I thought I heard- made the world stop spinning. Elijah ran off the road, flipped his car and went through the windshield. I got physically cold. My body tightened and I started praying. "Jehovah Rapha, please save my Son. Let him live, God. Be there with him while I'm not." I started praying in the spirit and calling Family and just rushing to get to the hospital. The ambulance arrived and he was covered in blood and in a neck brace, but he was talking and smiling. I couldn't immediately go back, but moments later (that seemed like an eternity) I pulled back the curtain and saw his beat up face and just cried.

"Can I kiss him?" I asked the nurse. She said "yes."

Elijah's first words to me I will NEVER forget... "It's ok Mom, God had me!"

Sheesh!! What the enemy meant for evil, our God turned it for good!!! I want you to know, I heard wrong. Elijah did not flip his car. But he did hit a tree, spun around and his head went through the windshield. No broken bones, no brain bleed, no brain swelling- nothing but 4 stitches in his head and glass that we picked out of his scalp for two weeks. Our God is a miracle worker- I don't doubt one second that Elijah had angels on assignment from God to protect him.

Remember that second request before I got in the water, that night in September? Revival in my Family...God has begun something in us and I know He will be faithful to complete it. Family devotions have been taking place every single night--we rotate between each of us so everyone has a chance to lead. It's creating a bond and a new thing because

Christ Jesus is FIRST again. I have one more request of the Lord, that I know can only happen if HE does it. But HE has been faithful all my life. So I know HE will be faithful again. In the words of a distant friend, Jasmine Brady, "He always comes through." I hope after reading all these intimate things of my life, you feel encouraged that God has a plan for your life, that is filled with GOOD. Bumps may come, but if you turn to Him and surrender, like really give it all to Him amazing things you will do!!!

    -Ashley

## Story Six: Joy Through the Valleys

Initially when my friend Laura asked me to write about a time that God was good in my life, I really struggled to think of something. Eventually, I realized that it wasn't one specific time but it was always. Through my childhood traumas, my failed relationships, and any turbulent time I have ever had, God was always there. I was on a divine path.

I am at a beautiful place in my life now, but it hasn't always been that way. I don't know that I ever wondered if God was there or not but looking back I can definitely see that he was. "Everything happens for a reason" sounds so cliché but there is a lesson to be learned from every bump and bruise. Hindsight is often 20/20, and it doesn't always seem easy to trust in those dark moments but those dark moments are often what propel us to the next level and help us become the best versions of ourselves.

On April 1st, 2021, my dad passed away. Losing a parent is not easy, but good can come even from seasons like these, full of loss and uncertainty. Growing up, my dad made sure to give my brother and me a childhood where the simple things in life were what we received, and he added a strong dose of love and affection to go along with that. He taught us integrity-- how to love all people and be compassionate, no matter someone else's circumstances-- but to always stand up for what was right.

When Laura spoke at my dad's funeral she talked about the meaning of my dad's name, Dale, which was "valley." She spoke about how he had lots of valleys in his life but he also had peaks. His valleys were his own seasons of uncertainty and loss, but his peaks included giving back to people all over the world by building houses through Habitat for Humanity in places as far away as Romania. If it weren't for the valleys, none of us would be able to get to the peak.

-Melissa

## Story Seven: Joy through an Answered Prayer

My family has attended and served at Rivertree Church since 2018. We had felt a pull to move from Henderson County to Daviess County for a while; but after all the chaos and confusion of our previous move, we were hesitant to deal with realtors and bank loans again.

In 2021, my husband Joe got a job in Owensboro at a factory. Our new insurance moved most of our family's appointments to Daviess County. Joe and I spent time sending each other links to other homes and properties in Daviess county, but nothing had really inspired us to pack up the house and contact a realtor. I would see bigger houses with more features on real estate apps and started to struggle with being content with my own home. I told the Lord I wanted to learn to be content with where we lived and not compare our home to other homes. So we invested in making our home beautiful and completed updates like a new metal roof, quartz countertops, updated landscape, and painting.

We loved our home, but still felt the pull to move towards Daviess County near our church family. In 2023, our church started to run with a vision to start a CrossFit gym to minister to the youth in Owensboro. During the meeting, I felt really strongly that I needed to be involved in this project and felt that the "yes" on my heart for the outreach was also a "yes" to move forward in positioning our family in Daviess county to be fully invested in ministry at Rivertree.

I felt that even though we were very involved in serving at church, there was still an element of disconnect because of the physical distance of where we lived. So in the spring of 2022, we used some of our tax money to have some trees in our front yard removed. I contacted a friend who removed trees to raise money for outreach events. I remember going outside after the first day he was on the job and looked up at the remaining trees. I very clearly heard the Lord say, "How much more money are you going to sink into this place before you do what I've asked you to do?" My heart started racing. I told the Lord, "We've already agreed to this tree removal job and the amount we would pay him. If we move, we can use this money for earnest money and moving expenses; but I can't screw this man out of the deal we've already made. If you really want us to move, give me wisdom on how to do this." He said, "If you start now, you can celebrate Christmas in your new home."

I talked to my husband and told him what I heard the Lord say. Joe was in agreement with the decision to move. I was very nervous, but I messaged our tree guy and told him what had happened. I asked him if there was any way that he could finish the trees he had already started and only charge us for that so we could use the remaining money for moving expenses. I apologized for being so unconventional and if he did not want to alter the original deal, we would stick with the original agreement and continue with the full job.

I waited anxiously for his reply. He responded very graciously and agreed to finish the trees he had already started and charged us less than half of what our original agreement was. He said, "I've found that many times when God asks us to do things, it is usually unconventional and I commend you for your obedience." We now had money for a storage pod and earnest money for our future home! The Lord honored our obedience and gave us favor with this man! We began decluttering and packing up the house for showings. We knew we wouldn't be able to move without the money from the sale of our current home, so we packed up in faith that God would open up the right home for us at the right time. Our church family is chock-full of talented people, so we used a realtor, a loan officer, and an insurance agent from our own church.

We felt that they all had our best interest in mind and were kingdom-minded individuals. Our realtor went above and beyond for us and showed us several properties that interested us–she and her husband even spent a Sunday morning looking for our septic tank (that we had been unable to find) on the new property so that we could have an inspection and she completed our contract for the new home while she was on vacation. Our loan officer was very straightforward and flexible with us. He explained things simply and the whole application process went smoothly. Our insurance agent was very efficient and explained terms and options in a way that I could easily understand.

Our team beautifully advocated and supported us during this transition. We had several people come to see the Spottsville house. It was a very stressful season to keep the house immaculate with four young children. We received positive and negative feedback. It was hard not to take the negative comments about our home personally, and I struggled with bouts of discouragement and doubt. One Sunday before going to see two properties with our realtor, our pastor told me about a property for sale that he saw while out running around his "neighborhood."

We didn't have an exact address, so Joe and I drove around Utica near our pastor's property and finally found the "for sale by owner" sign! We got out to look around outside and fell in love with the property! It was a double-wide manufactured home on 1-acre of land with three storage buildings. I started to daydream about creating a homestead on this property and contacted the owner. He was a very kind, down-to-earth guy who agreed to show us inside the home the following Sunday.

Our pastor agreed to check it out with us. We fell in love with the property and home. One of the storage buildings was actually finished with drywall, electricity, and a wood burning stove. I imagined it to be a one-room schoolhouse for our homeschool. Joe and I both agreed to put in an offer. Our offer was accepted and we were under contract. One week later, we received several offers for our home and were under contract ourselves. We were then able to schedule inspections and appraisals for our dream property while our buyers scheduled inspections for our Spottsville home. The inspections for the new house didn't have any surprises and went fairly smoothly. However, the inspection for our Spottsville home had lots of surprises. The exact same inspection company did the home inspection for our buyers that we used when we bought the property in 2015. We did not change anything with the crawlspace or attic but were given lots of negative feedback regarding those areas. Our septic tank inspection required repair work. Our buyers backed out of the deal before we even got a chance to offer remediation.

    I struggled with so much shame and embarrassment. I felt so discouraged–not only because our contract fell through and we might lose the new property, but I felt that our team and others would think that we were dishonest. If I had known any of those things had been an issue, we wouldn't have listed our home until we were able to address those things. I had some very real conversations with the Lord, "Why did you have me do this if it wasn't going to happen? What's the point of all this?" I felt like we wouldn't be able to get out from under all of these issues and accusations. We had friends who just a few years earlier had their home sell within 72 hours after listing and I had faith that we could have the same testimony. I was obeying the Lord, after all. Why shouldn't we have the same results as them?

I was comparing our story to others' stories and it was stealing my joy. I talked to my pastor who is experienced in construction and my realtor who has home renovation experience. They were able to give us manageable solutions in addressing our inspection issues. We had the septic tank repaired and took steps to remediate the inspection issues over the weekend. Our home had several more showings when placed back on the market, but it seemed that nobody was interested in making an offer.

I finally had enough with feeling discouraged and one day while I was loading the kids up to leave for another showing, I turned and declared out loud into my living room: "This is the Lord's house. He gave us this house and he will move us when He is ready. I will not be moved by the way our circumstances look. If we stay here, the Lord is good. If we move, the Lord is good. We will obey the Lord, even when we feel foolish or discouraged. This house belongs to Him, not me." I left with my kids and had a strange peace for the remainder of the moving process. We were under contract within a week! The new buyer was a realtor himself. He knew going into the deal what the previous inspections said and the repairs we had made. He made us a great offer that allowed us to move forward to our new property in Daviess County. It took exactly three months from the day we listed to the day we closed, but the Lord provided and opened doors for us every step of the way. It was a time of learning to trust the Lord through uncertainty. He is faithful.

-Hannah

## Story Eight: Love, Healing and His Goodness

I never considered, or thought it possible, to experience God's goodness amidst adversity and pain. However, I have experienced His goodness through many adversities, it was a matter of me changing my perspective. I would have never survived if it wasn't for the love and goodness of God. He used my adversities, dark nights of the soul, to make me into a woman of promise, a woman of love, a woman of integrity and a woman of purpose and destiny (to name a few).

In 1996, my husband (at the time) decided to file for divorce; I was heartbroken. He was the only man I had ever trusted and he chose to walk away when things got tough. to say I was devastated is an understatement. I attempted to take my life, but God had other plans for me. The next several years were difficult, I struggled with my emotional health and questioned who and where God was in all of this. I started an intimate relationship with another man, who turned out to have a drinking problem. Sometimes, when he drank too much he was abusive. He loved my good credit and my money. When the money ran out things became worse and I left him.

At this time, with the help of several of my sisters, I moved to North Carolina. This meant I left my two teenage sons behind with their dad, so I could focus on myself. I saw them once a month. This time away began my transformation, I began to focus on healing the loss of my marriage and my childhood trauma. When I returned home, I moved in with my sister until I could get my own apartment. God led me to a spirit-filled therapist that was instrumental in my healing and understanding the goodness of God in the face of pain, trauma and loss. God began to work in me, showing me traumas I had hidden away, as well as areas of my life where I had left satan rule and reign. The Lord showed me love, acceptance and the importance of letting others in. During this time, my divorce became final and my ex-husband remarried.

The Lord continued to show me love, healing and His goodness. I found an incredible, spirit-filled church that was supportive. Several of my sisters walked closely with me in this dark night of my soul. Jesus also provided me with several close friends. These individuals loved and supported me without judgement, showing me the goodness of God. Walking through the pain and loss was difficult, at times overwhelming, but it was worth it. It was the goodness of the

Most High God that sustained me and gave me the strength to persevere facing the many obstacles in my way and to grow in my relationship and intimacy with HIM.

-Shirl

## Story Nine: More than I Can Handle

You've heard the saying, "He'll never put anything on you that you can't handle." That statement has never settled cozily into my spirit. Some days are hard to handle. For instance, I remember a time after a long day at work, I would come home to a house full of boys who hadn't cleaned up after themselves. A little boy making a PB&J is really messy, and so is everything he touches. My hopes of joyfully resting after a long day turns into me cleaning up much of the house.

There were days where I couldn't seem to handle it! On the other hand, looking back, at least their schoolwork was always finished when I came home and they could make their own PB&J, so this momma has learned to choose her battles.

Just as some days are hard to handle, whole seasons can be hard to handle too. I've been through seasons of sadness. We've moved away from three different churches in three different states. Each transition meant leaving the relationships we loved so much, to temporarily live with family in a home that wasn't ours, until the next season began. Talk about hard to handle. It's difficult raising a family in someone else's home when you share a bathroom! I've also been through seasons of stretching. Shortly after we stepped into full time ministry, my husband started having seizures.

Those seizures lasted 11 years before we found a doctor who was determined to figure it all out. In 2016 he underwent two brain surgeries. It was hard to handle this season of not knowing if healing was possible, but with God, all things are possible. God stretched my faith in this season and as many of you know, my husband is now 4 years seizure free! That whole story, or testimony if you will, is a message all in itself. So, I want to reword that original statement that I first shared if you don't mind: "He'll never put anything on you **that you and He** can't handle." You see He may allow us to go through those hard-to-handle things, so we realize our need for Him.

In the book of 1 Samuel, we meet a shepherd boy named David. He was minding his own business, and his sheep too, when his dad, Jessie, invited him to meet the prophet, Samuel. Of course, this invitation was only reluctantly extended to David after his 7 older brothers failed to meet God's confirmation to be anointed king. God was not searching for the outer appearance like man does – he was looking for the heart. When David walks in with his pure heart, the horn of oil is brought out, and he is anointed king of Israel. Although it was likely a beautiful moment of awe for his dad, and a hilarious look of shock from his brothers, David returned to the field to tend to his sheep. From that moment until he actually sits on the throne, David walks through many trying seasons himself. From shepherding sheep, to playing the harp, to dodging spears, he had to walk through a wilderness before God allowed him to sit on a throne.

You see, we are all called according to our purpose and our purpose requires preparation. Guess what, preparation is sometimes hard to handle! Yet, it's our highs and lows in life that prepare us for tomorrow.

For every success David had in Saul's eye, and for every time he had to flee, I bet David didn't necessarily feel like he was walking out an anointing to be king. He was just doing the next right thing. Unknowingly to him, that next right thing was preparation in God's plan. For every right thing David did, he had a "He and me" mindset, as he always found his strength in the Lord.

Right now, maybe your next right step is to stand firm in your "right now," no matter how big or small. It makes me think of Noah from the Notebook, when he was standing firm in a "right now" moment he pleaded with Allie, "So, it's not going to be easy. It's going to be really hard. We're going to have to work at this every day, but I want to do that because I want you..."

Hard to handle times, whether days or seasons, are an inevitable part of life. They are going to come no matter what. It's our posture in those times that displays our willingness to trust the Lord. Will we fall and not get up? Or will we stand like David and say, "The battle is the Lord's!"

There's nothing you and He can't handle.
-Jodie

## Story Ten: Even When I Feel Alone

"God is good all the time and all the time God is good." This is a very common phrase that I have heard my whole life. I believe it and agree that it is true but sometimes it can be hard to see the goodness of God in certain moments or periods of time in life. I think sometimes as Christians, or at least myself, can tend to notice the goodness of God more when everything is going right. When there's blessing, provision at the moment it's needed, healing that comes quickly, supernatural intervention in a split second that you didn't even know you needed until after it came. I have plenty of those kinds of testimonies throughout the years of my relationship with Jesus. But, the testimony I want to share is about a time that God was good in my life recently, when I felt like every single part of my life, spiritually and physically, was shifting and changing and it felt like a very dark time emotionally. However, even in those moments and seasons of life, the goodness of God is still all around us, His presence is still with us, and we can find Him in the midst of chaos.

Around the beginning of May last year I began to feel the shift that I mentioned above. Our oldest son was heading back out to staff a missions school, something he's done the last two years. Our oldest daughter was graduating high school and was preparing to leave for six months in the fall for the same missions school. Our youngest son had just turned 16, this was very hard for me because I realized that he was getting older and gaining more independence, which meant he was inching even closer to graduation and finding his own path just like the other two. Our youngest daughter was almost 11 and about to start her middle school years.

    These are all good things, and while I have been a stay at home mom for the entirety of their lives and have homeschooled all of them, it seemed that suddenly my role in their lives was so different. The way they needed me was much different than when they were all younger. They still needed me but I was struggling with this transition into pre-teen, teen, and adulthood. Some of that is normal emotions that would be expected. Change is hard and can be tricky to navigate. But this was deeper for me. It felt like I suddenly didn't know who I was. My identity and calling, if you will, had been wrapped up in what I had done the past several years and when that began to shift, I emotionally felt wrecked. And at the same time,

God was also shifting things spiritually for me.

Asking me to step out in new ways to minister to others, to speak about different topics at women's events, to write and share personal prayers that I had intended to stay hidden in my journal. This was hard for me because Jesus was shattering my comfort zone and testing my trust in Him. These times of life aren't uncommon, many, if not all of us, have had times where we feel contradicting emotions coexisting with each other, and this time in my life I was living in a dual state of sadness and happiness. Sadness because of all the change and new things that felt challenging, but happiness in celebrating all of their milestone moments. I was genuinely excited for the growth and achievements that my kids were experiencing.

That's the testimony here-- that the goodness of God was still all around me in one of the darkest times emotionally for me during those few months. It wasn't that there were terrible things happening. Outside looking in, there were many exciting and celebratory events going on. It was the stuff in my heart that Jesus, in His kindness, was dealing with. My need to control and be the "fixer of all things" instead of trusting God to do what only He can do. My unhealthy view of my actual role in my kids' lives, which is to raise them to know God and

release them for Him to lead and guide. My wanting to stay in my comfort zone and avoid any
and all stretching in the arena of ministry or new things God was asking of me.

So many emotions and moments I felt like I was losing it mentally. But you know what? God met me in those places! Every time I cried (and screamed) out to Him in prayer, His peace came. Every time I had no words to pray or express what I was feeling, only tears, I could feel His nearness like a friend sitting in silence with me just being there. He was putting pieces of my heart back together with the glue of His love. Every time I felt it was silly and I was being dramatic to be experiencing sorrow and mourning because of all of the changes, that were actually good things in life, He reminded me that my journey is MY journey and my story is MY story and HE doesn't see me as silly or dramatic, which began to heal the negative thoughts and words I spoke over myself and thought that others were speaking as well.

Every time I felt overwhelmed by the thought of stepping out into a new opportunity, He empowered me to say "yes" and face more fears that needed to be conquered. ALL of these examples that I lived in and fought through for a season were times that the goodness of God came rushing in and surrounded me the way I needed. My heart now resonates even more with the truth that "God is good all the time and all the time God is good." His goodness doesn't waiver! Sometimes it's on display in big extravagant ways and sometimes we just have to look a little closer and deeper into situations to see it.

   -Elisha

## Story Eleven: Deep Roots of Faith

When asked to share my testimony about a time that God has been good to me, I can't think of a time that he hasn't been good to me. He formed me in the womb, created me in his image, and he knows the number of hairs on my head- he loves me!

At the age of six, I began to understand and inquire about salvation and started seeking the Lord in my life. I read the Bible regularly and prayed daily. I felt that I was missing something in my life. I didn't understand what God was doing but I felt an eagerness to seek him. I'll never forget the night I gave my life to the Lord. I felt the Holy Spirit so strong tugging at my heart. As a nine year old, I knelt near my great grandmother's bedside and I gave my life to the Lord. I understood what it meant to a Christian and I wanted to feel true peace. The same peace that I saw within her.

I was raised in a Christ-centered home, where attending church was what we did as a family. At that point, church was more of a routine and I didn't have a personal relationship with the Lord. My family attended a small country church founded by my great grandfather. Most attendees were relatives, including the pastor, my great uncle.

My great grandmother was a faithful member in the church. She made a lasting impact on my life. She was a Proverb 31 woman that loved the Lord and fully committed to serving and giving what little she had to the Lord. She was a woman of no wealth but truly had it all. She had pure joy, contentment, and set such a great example to follow. She loved and feared the Lord. God used my great grandmother's obedience and walk to touch many lives around her, including mine.

I felt the Lord's calling on my life at age twelve to serve in missions but I wasn't sure what that entailed. I felt my purpose was to serve where God called me and at that time, God opened doors for me to assist in the kids' church. I always had a passion to work with younger children. I knew I wanted to work with children in some capacity in my adult years. Little did I know that God was molding and shaping me to his will, his plan, and purpose for my life- teaching children. God was equipping me to minister to children.

It wasn't long after I felt called that the Lord closed that door and that was a hard season to understand. I was asked to step down from helping because I wasn't a fit for the church. I didn't attend a Christian school or wear dresses as my everyday attire. Even though I felt God called me, I was told I was no longer needed. Although I was broken inside, I felt the closeness of God. He was near to my broken heart. Thankfully, this gave me more of a burning desire to seek the Lord and I am thankful that God's faithfulness kept the desire within my heart. Sometimes our path can be hard to understand, it can be hurtful and confusing at times, but God had a purpose and his plan is far better than mine.

I later attended another church where God put me in a youth group where I was blessed to attend church camp. This helped me in my walk and drew me closer to God and he was equipping me to navigate my teenage years. As an adult, I've been blessed to serve in different capacities within the church. From food pantry ministry, teaching Mission friends, Middle School Sunday School teacher, Kindergarten/First grade Sunday School teacher to High school small group leader, etc. I have been blessed to serve where God has called me. I have learned to always follow God and he has made my path straight.

I've often felt inadequate in ministry and have had my share of doubts, but through Christ, the Lord has always been there to uplift me. After all, the Lord equips the called. God has always met every need, heard every prayer, seen every heartbreak, and has been a faithful, good father. I'm not sure where I'd be without him. I am thankful for his calling upon my life and his continual grace he has shown me.

For years, I was searching to find my way, my path, my joy, and peace for my life. Trying to determine my title, my role, my place; I worried needlessly about my identity as a person. It wasn't until my thirties, that I realized my most important identity was in Christ and not my own. I didn't need a title, an abbreviation before or after my name, a label, etc., I had Christ within me- that's all I needed. I am just an ordinary girl who had Christ living within me. Turning to Christ and fully committing my life is where I find rest, inner peace, and true joy! When I learned to put Jesus first, others next, then myself- I found the true J-O-Y! I have been blessed with the title I was seeking- a believer of the Lord Jesus Christ! He created me in his image, gave me purpose, and called me to serve in missions and I am thankful he chose me. Jeremiah 29:11

God has given me the desires of my heart and I couldn't be more thankful. I am a teacher at a private Christian school and I'm able to share my faith daily with children. Our school is comparable to a mission field. In fact, half our students are unchurched and consider our school Chapel as their church. Chapel is their favorite special of the week as well as mine! It brings me joy seeing children worship and have such eagerness to learn about God. I am blessed to have the opportunity to share the good news! God is moving within our school and several have come to salvation- Praise God! Please, continue to pray for our staff as well as myself as we share about God.

I don't have a radical testimony, but what I've come to know is that my identity is in the Lord. He brings me true joy and has equipped me with his calling on my life. I have a burning desire to live for the Lord, to witness, and to love people. To God be the glory for leading, guiding, and directing my path. I have seen the goodness of God!

-Natalie

## Story Twelve: A Touch of Real Love

*Ecclesiastes 3:11 "God has made everything beautiful in its time."*

I surrendered my life to the Lord shortly after turning 30. Up to that point, I had made a lifestyle out of running from my pain. My life had been marked by brokenness from my childhood and I had run out of places to hide.

Jesus met me at the end of a very dark and lonely season when I had finally come to the end of myself. I was broken, alone, single, never been married and without any children. I was desperate for a touch of real love. Love that could only come from Him. I became a new creation inside His love.

As I began to walk with Him, he healed pieces of me. He allowed me to dream with Him about my future and my desires. I had been in survival mode for so long, unable to see or know what I truly wanted in life. As my eyes opened to the possibilities, I realized that more than anything, I wanted to be a wife and mother. These were the very things I had run from for so long yet here I was desiring them!

I had been scared that I would pass along the brokenness and trauma I had carried to my future children. BUT GOD! He is faithful and His timing is perfect. I began to ask Him for a husband and children. It was hard at first, but I started to believe that He would answer me. I made a list of attributes that I desired in a husband and prayed over it. At almost 34 years old, it seemed like a long shot, but not for God! He gave me the desire of my heart, and I met my husband that year!

On my journey with the Lord, He continued to heal me in deep places to prepare me for His promises. He blessed us with 3 beautiful children. There are many days that I can hardly believe this is my life. Had He given me the desire of my heart any earlier in life, I would not have been prepared to receive it.

His goodness and mercy mean that our children are growing up in a home full of love and righteousness. My children will not know the pain of generational trauma. They are being raised to truly know God so they will be equipped early to walk in their destinies. Children of faith are intentionally raised and discipled. The grace to wait upon the Lord will bless my family for generations to come.

Proverbs 22:6 "Train up a child in the way he should go; and when he is old he will not depart from it."

-Ashley R.

## Story Thirteen: Joy Through Healing

I once was a little girl who was fighting for my life time and time again. Now there is a peaceful ease where there once was pain, anger and struggle. The Lord blessed me with so many miracles in my life, but one stands to tell of it time and time again. That is how the Lord took my pain and struggle, defeat and anger into triumph and victory to whole and set free.

When I was five years old, I was diagnosed with Pancreatitis, a rare disease for children, but most common for adults. The doctors had discovered that my pancreas had two ducts where there is only supposed to be one. I had to have my first surgery to remove the tip of the tail at age five, due to that tip being dead. After that, I would endure two more surgeries called Pancreaticojejunostomy in which they reroute parts of my pancreas and other organs. Those surgeries did not work and I had to endure more pancreatic attacks and hospital stays. I never once lost my faith in the Lord, I knew he was going to continue to take care of me. I was going to continue to take care of myself. I was told as a young child I would not live to be 18 years old. That was devastating news for my parents and myself.

I was told as a teenager that I may not be able to have children, but boy did God have other plans for me. Nolan Lee Edge came into this world June 20, 2013 and filled my heart with so much joy and happiness. I still continued to have many hospital stays and now I had to miss being with my son. My faith still never wavered and I prayed for healing and understood only in his time. On May 26, 2016, my life changed in so many ways. This was the fourth time I had surgery to remove my entire pancreas.

Yes, I was a little scared because I wasn't sure how my life was going to look. I knew though the Lord and savior had me in the palm of his hand. While in surgery, my doctor Michael West found the head of my pancreas was still working and viable. Of course, after surgery I did endure a lot of pain but I suffered through it because I knew something greater was in store. I did have to go to rehab for 12 days in August of 2016 due to being on pain meds for almost 8 years straight. This was one of the best decisions I ever made! I was free from pain of the pancreatitis and free from relying on the opioids and having a constant want for them. I no longer had pancreatitis. I was healed and made new.

To some, it may be just an ordinary surgery, one that doctors perform all the time. May 26, 2016 will forever be a day that me and my family will always remember. Matthew 17:20 says "faith as small as a mustard seed can move a mountain." I never, ever let my faith go to the Lord. I knew that in his timing, with his unfailing love, and his grace and mercy, that I would be made whole again. I would be set apart for something greater in this thing called life. The Lord gave me a second chance to live life to the fullest, to count my blessings every single day and to remember that the Lord made me tiny, but he made me oh so mighty!

-Katie

## Story Fourteen: Bigger than a Diagnosis

God is always good even when we don't see it. He asks, even commands, us to walk by faith not knowing the outcome, but fully trusting in Him to see us through to victory whatever that looks like. We must walk forward even when we feel like a five-ton weight is staking our feet to the ground. We plow into the scary unknown with Him by our side, even carrying us when we feel weak.

To set the scene, this journey of faith began at Texas Roadhouse in May 2023. What I thought was a date night changed drastically when Donald's smiling expression dropped and told me his blood test had showed an abnormal spike of an "M" protein in his blood. His physician recommended finding an oncologist to continue testing. Because my husband is a researcher, he already had an exhaustive study of possible diagnoses, percentages of possibilities with each diagnosis, possible treatments and survival rates. Quite frankly, it was frightening. My only reaction was tears. I had no words, just tears. We set out to find a doctor, and my prayer life intensified greatly. We told very

few people as we began this journey of faith and doubt. We chose to share only with those
who we knew would only speak life and refuse the instant negativity that comes with the "C" word. This is what we felt God required of us. We later found out this was biblical because Jesus did not share the raising of Jairus's daughter with everyone–just a few. We couldn't have unbelief from others through hindering words being spoken. We wanted life-giving words only.

    The following weeks were filled with ups and downs. Each test brought less than positive results, but we continued to speak only words of faith in healing. Many times, my faith wavered, but we decided we could only speak life even though our lives, our world, was crumbling beneath us. All kinds of thoughts crossed my mind. How would I survive? How could we even afford the treatments–treatments would financially drain us? However, God is bigger than any diagnosis and all of my doubts.

    For weeks Don would go to work, and I would spend 2 hours a day sitting at our church crying, praying, reading words of faith and healing from the Bible, and decreeing into the atmosphere that Donald would be healed and fulfill his Kingdom destiny. One particular morning I was reading Isaiah; I can't even recall what verses. All I truly remember about the moments before was that I was at a very low moment in this journey. My faith wasn't where it needed it to survive. I sat with tears dropping onto the pages of the Bible sitting open across my lap. I felt a prick in my heart to look at my Bible.

When I looked down, I saw blue words, " I will heal him" literally jump off the page. It was as if the words had come alive and leaped off the page. In the moment, I remember the overwhelming sense of peace and relief that God was going to answer our prayers, and He had given me a tangible sign. The words of encouragement bolstered my faith: my husband would have a long healthy life and fulfill all that God has for him. If I hadn't experienced this myself, I don't know that I would have believed this was possible.

As I relaxed and became less emotional, I began to search for the words I had seen in the Spirit. I scoured the pages of Isaiah for blue words. I knew God had sent a special message to renew my faith and give peace that only He can give. The scripture that I found was from Isaiah 57:18-19 KJV. "I have seen his ways, and will heal him: I will lead him also, and restore comforts unto him and his mourners. I will create the fruit of the lips; Peace, peace to him that is far off, and to him that is near, saith the Lord; and I will heal him." These words in my Bible were not blue nor highlighted in blue, they were highlighted in pink, so the experience was truly an encounter with my very personal amazing Savior who was walking through this agonizing journey with us. He had heard our cries and was answering our prayers. I felt I had a word straight from heaven.

From that day, the burden wasn't lighter, but we had a new sense of peace and grace abounding in our lives. We knew God was going to do something miraculous. We didn't know when, where, or how, but we knew in our hearts we were about to tangibly see the hand of God moving in our lives. With a new sense of hope, we traveled to the fourth appointment to receive the results from the bone marrow biopsy. The Nurse practitioner, totally unprepared for the visit, scanned the results from each of the tests Don had. She then delivered her diagnosis–multiple myeloma, cancer of the plasma cells–and we needed to start treatment immediately. She suggested chemotherapy which may or may not prolong his life.

At the moment she stopped speaking, something rose in me that I cannot explain. I simply sat unmoving in my seat and said, "We do not come into agreement with your diagnosis." She looked perplexed and responded with, "Yes, you should get a second opinion." But that wasn't the appropriate response to my statement. "No, you don't understand. Our God is bigger than your diagnosis." We didn't and wouldn't come into agreement with her death sentence. We refused to accept her words into our lives. Our next 45 minutes in that office were an incredible visitation from God for this nurse practitioner. Don stood and stated, "We are here today because God wanted to reach you. He used this situation in our lives for you." We had been on assignment to remind this young lady who God had called her to be. (This is a whole different story in itself.)

We left the oncology office and called my cousin in Nashville looking for a doctor who would walk with us during this spiritual journey. Through a divine series of events, we had a new spirit-filled doctor in Gallatin, Tennessee, within 24 hours. She arranged for a PET scan and had Donald's records transferred thus beginning the second leg of our journey. The days following the PET scan were tense and emotional. The technicians said the test would take 2 hours, but Don had finished in 45 minutes. That was a good sign, right? Days turned into weeks, and we still hadn't heard from the doctor about the results of the PET scan. When Don would mention it, I simply would answer, "No news is good news." Still, we waited for confirmation from the doctor's phone call. I assume the wait was getting to Donald, so he began searching on the internet to find a way to see his

results. He finally found the website that offered a connection to his personal medical records. Don checked for his scan results, and all three images read 0%, 0%, and 0%. God had answered our prayers but still no confirmation from the doctor's office.

    We finally called the doctor's office to schedule an appointment to get our results. The receptionist apologized for the delay but said they didn't call less-critical patients as quickly as those who had serious

issues. At the appointment, the doctor confirmed what we had read on his chart, no cancer. She wanted to watch him over the next year or so but agreed that God had healed Donald. We had experienced a miracle–God had healed him just as he had said.

    For the rest of the year, Don and I would travel to Gallatin to take blood and urine tests to reaffirm the new life sentence God had given. With each visit, Don's numbers have improved. God is faithful to do all that He promised: He is our healer.

    -Trish

## Story Fifteen: The Other Side of Addiction

At almost thirty-two years old, It's literally a miracle I'm alive. I started to use drugs starting at the age of 17 and by the time I turned 21, I was a heavy drug user. I'd do anything I could get my hands on it to escape how I felt inside. I struggled on and off for several more years-- Meth, Heroin, pills, Fentanyl I've done it all. I've done things I never in my life thought I would do. I've been in situations I know for a fact that God's hand was on me, or I would have died.

During those years I lived with my grandma, and some would say she enabled me, but my grandma truly loved me. She prayed for me constantly. It didn't matter if it was 2 o'clock in the morning, day or night my grandma was opening her door for me. When everyone else shut me out, my grandma stood beside me, whether I was wrong or right. But she ALWAYS let me know when I was wrong. If it wasn't for God, and the grandmother I had, I would have never made it out of my addiction alive.

I had Atticus when I was 25, and my grandma and my mom helped me raise him until I got sober. In 2020, I overdosed and was unstable for 18 hours. I will never forget waking up in the hospital screaming for my little boy. I didn't understand how someone could love their kid as much as I did, but continue abandoning them for drugs. Shortly after overdosing on Heroin and making another promise to myself and everyone around me that I would never use it again, I ended up back in the hospital two weeks later. I tripped so bad on Acid; I went to hell on my trip. (That's another story for another time) I ended up getting sober after that for a year. I was really trying to stay that way; I was doing so good. I was sober, had my own place, had custody of my son, making good money at my Job and then BOOM. RELAPSE. This relapse took me to the lowest place in my life I had ever been. PURE MISERY... "From heaven you sent a fire that burned in my bones; you set a trap for my feet, and you made me turn back. All day long you leave me in shock from constant pain." Lamentations 1:13 This scripture describes exactly how I felt.

 I had PTSD from tripping Acid. A year before this relapse when I went to Hell, I would have panic attacks thinking the world was going to end. My whole body would feel like it would catch fire, my walls would look like they were melting, my boyfriend literally thought I was nuts. I called my dad early one morning and told him he needed to come to my house. I was having a panic attack so bad, I knew that's what it was but because of everything I was going through I needed him to come talk me out of my panic. My dad pulled scripture out of the bible explaining to me that God wanted me to pick a side, that I could no longer continue living the way I was, In total darkness. It was later either that evening or sometime that week I remember crying out to the Lord. I said, "God If you're real, HELP ME!"

I've been to every treatment center in Owensboro and the surrounding counties, I've had sponsors, I've worked steps, I've literally tried it all and could never get sober and stay sober. Even the times I got sober, I would have reservations to use. This relapse lasted almost a year. I remember the same night I packed my bags to go back to my grandma's to try to get sober, someone kicked my door in. "No weapon formed against you shall prosper, and every tongue that rises against you in judgement you shall condemn" Isaiah 54:14 (This is a verse that my grandma would pray over me since I was a small child.)

The devil tried to take me out countless times and never succeeded. Two weeks after I cried out to the Lord, He removed every desire to use. I went from digging in my veins to digging in the word of God. God completely transformed my life. When I first got clean my mouth was full of foul language. I remember asking God to help me to quit cussing, He told me to read the book of James. I'm telling you he did it, he washed me clean. It's been three years since I've used drugs.

Remember me saying I lived with my grandma on and off through my addiction? During that time, we lived on Sunset Drive. God doesn't miss a beat. He sees and knows it all. My grandma was my best friend. I got pregnant with my daughter, and honestly, I was so scared. My whole pregnancy I was depressed. My grandma pushed me through my hard days all while she was battling lung cancer. Bless her heart.

We had decided on a name for my daughter after nine long months of really not knowing. I wasn't totally set on the name until after I had her. I knew then that's why God had given us the name for her. The same exact night I went in to have Sunny, my grandma was passing over to heaven. I didn't know until several hours after I had my Babygirl. I had been trying to Facetime my grandma all morning to show her my precious little girl. As My grandma's life here on earth was setting, God gave me Sunny. "Weeping may come for the night but joy comes in the morning" Psalm 30:5

God knew exactly what I needed to push me through my grandma's death. Not to say it hasn't hurt. This last year has been one of the hardest but most bittersweet years I've ever had to process and without God's grace and mercy, it wouldn't have been possible. A year later, I can look back on my whole life and see where God has been in every single detail. He's so faithful and his mercies are new each morning. My best advice to anyone, if you're struggling with ANYTHING, don't be ashamed. Cry out to Jesus, God is your ultimate healer.

-Krislyn

## Story Sixteen: Embracing His Plan

Embrace: the act of holding someone closely in one's arms; the act of accepting or supporting something willingly or enthusiastically. It's also my word for 2025.

When Laura asked me to share my testimony, I kind of laughed at first. Although I was honored that she even thought of me, I shrank back, feeling unworthy and insufficient. I want to be an encouragement to others, and I want to glorify God for all that he's done and is doing in my life. *But why me? I'm not good enough, and my story isn't special.* Before telling Laura *no*, I decided I should pray about it first. Honestly, I believed God would make it clear to me that I had no business telling others about Him. My life is chaotic and messy! But God had other plans…

So I'm stepping out in faith and following God's call for me. I'm embracing this opportunity. I still struggle with feelings of inadequacy, but I know God doesn't call the qualified, He qualifies the called. 2020 was a rough year. The last few months of 2020 were especially difficult for my family and me. In September I got Covid. I battled the sickness at home for a week or two before my husband and my dad decided I needed to see a doctor.

When I arrived at the hospital, my oxygen was in the 70s, and I was immediately moved to the hospital's covid-unit where I spent the next week in isolation.

In November, my family and I were on our way to get breakfast before heading to my daughter's softball tournament when someone ran a red-light and blindsided us. Two of my daughters had to be transported by ambulance to the children's hospital for treatment and my car was totaled. But by the grace of God, we all survived 2020.

2020 was the most difficult time of my life, but I experienced God's presence in ways I never could have imagined. I was reminded that His strength is made perfect through my weakness. The challenges I faced not only deepened my faith but also shaped my perspective on what truly matters. I was reminded of the importance of living each day with purpose and intention.

My purpose for being here is to love people the way Jesus loves me, and I intend for my life to be a reflection of His grace, mercy, and compassion. As Jesus said in Matthew 25:40, "Truly I tell you, whatever you did for one of the least of these brothers and sisters of mine, you did for me." And that's the verse that inspires me. I want to see every act of kindness, no matter how small, as an opportunity to serve Him and reflect His love to others. This call to love and serve led me to Borrowed Hearts, a local nonprofit that desires to be the hands and feet of Jesus by equipping and empowering foster families. When I first learned of Borrowed Hearts, I knew it was an opportunity to put my faith into action.

By volunteering and supporting this ministry, I've been able to experience the joy of serving children and families who are walking through challenging seasons, and I've seen firsthand how God can use ordinary people like me to make an extraordinary impact.

Through every trial and triumph in my life, God has been faithful. He's taught me that my story—no matter how chaotic and messy—is a testament to His goodness and grace.

As I look ahead to 2025, I'm committed to willingly and enthusiastically embracing every person and every opportunity God places before me, and I will do so with confidence—not in myself but in the One who goes before me. I pray that each of us will step out in faith and embrace the unique call God has placed on our lives.

-Brooke

## Story Seventeen: My God Story

I grew up going to church on Sundays in the winter when it was cold outside and there was nothing to be done outside. We never talked about God, or grace or sinning. Just basically sang age old hymns and recited some doctrines. I knew nothing about grace. I didn't understand the concept. I didn't have a personal relationship with Jesus.

My very young parents separated when I was just an infant. Never did I understand the impact that had on my life. Fathers don't leave their children. They protect them, guard them, insure their safety. Mine
did not. I felt abandoned. I craved attention as a child. My mother remarried and worked hard to provide opportunities for me. I was a step-child. I did all the things I was supposed to do as a teen. I made good grades, stayed out of trouble for the most part, and made it look like I kept it all together. I was FCA President and a member of the National Junior Honor Society. I got into Vanderbilt.

But what my parents didn't know was that I was hurting. I was seeking love and attention from friends and boys all through school. I kept on attempting to find value and recognition in the things of this world. Even on days I thought I had really excelled, no one seemed to notice.

When my father was in my life, he was over the top. Happy one minute, screaming at me the next. I craved his approval more than anything but I could never seem to please him. No matter what I did, I could never please him. So I kept trying, as did my step-mom, and his other children. His expectations were so high. Even when I thought I was close, it never seemed like enough. I was trying to gain his love through actions.

In high school, I went to FCA camp and met an incredible counselor there who was kind and caring, loving and full of what I saw to be God's grace. She was a cheerleader in college, had a sweet southern accent, and talked to me, for the first time in my life, about how much God loved me and how good He was to me. We sang beautiful praise music, held hands high and I committed myself to God.

Fast forward, a few Bible studies, Sunday school classes, a job where we prayed before every staff meeting, I was occasionally half-heartedly going through the motions, but still I did not feel different. If I worked hard and acted like everything would be fine, I looked like I had it all together, including my faith. But inside, I was empty, longing for something more, being pulled by something but not knowing what.

I knew I wanted my children in church. I knew it was the right thing. I wanted them to love it, to long for it. To know Bible stories I didn't know. I tried for a little while to take them on my own, but it was work. And I wasn't convicted. So life went on and I went back to school. Day after day, night after night of the grind. Constantly feeling behind and left out. And alone. Completely alone. No one to reach out to, no one to bring me out. Convinced by my dad that no one could ever understand what I was going through, so why would I even talk about it? Tired and lonely, depressed and anxious, I closed myself off to everyone, including God. Satan was happy. He is keen at pulling us into sin and then punishing us for it over and over until we continue to drown in his agony. I allowed it to happen. I allowed feelings of inadequacy and a desire for self-importance to suffocate me.

What had I given up, I thought? What rights had I delegated when I married at a young age? What opportunities had I forsaken to follow my husband's career? I longed for success, spotlight, glory. I wanted to be noticed, recognized, praised for all the things I had accomplished. And so I plunged myself into a relationship that was bad for me. It was bad for me. It brought me superficial recognition and shallow praise. It was empty and dark, and sick. And Satan had his victory. He filled my heart and head with lies of unforgiveness, failure, screaming at me that I would never recover from this sickness, from this disease I had created. And there I stayed, neck-deep in my own self-loathing and self-hatred, only wanting someone to reach out and rescue me from my miserable pit. I was who I had been afraid of becoming. The traitor, the liar, the fake, the mask. I was the

disappointment that I so wanted to avoid. I was unable to meet the expectations that were set for me. My identity was lost.

*The evil deeds of a wicked man ensnare him; the cords of his sin hold him fast. He will die for lack of discipline, led astray by his own great folly. Proverbs 5:22-23*

God called me gently at first, through the words and actions of my husband, I could see his hand reaching out to me from the corner of my eye. It was just barely there, and sometimes I couldn't see it

at all. There was a glimpse of something different in him, a new hope, a new awareness of what was happening, a calming. Day by day, week by week, God changed my heart. He showed me the error I had made, the lies I had believed, the devastation I had created. He also showed me his unchanging grace and love.

So what was my choice? To sink into myself, close my eyes and let the mud overtake me? Or reach up and grasp the hand that was being held out to me? And then what? What had happened to my life, the
lie that everything inside me was ok? The billboard picture of the smiling face that covered the mask of fear and shame? Do I run and hide or do I walk gently into the light? I walked slowly and timidly at first and then I ran toward the darkness, because just beyond the darkness is the dawn, and there is where I feel God's presence, His glory, His pride, not pride for things I have done but pride for the things I have learned, for the choice I have made to follow him and not to follow my own selfish desires. Never will I be perfect, but I am reconciled, and redeemed, I am washed free
from the blood of sin.

I do not have to live in denial or shame or self-loathing because Christ died for me, for my selfish, stupid, idiot moves and my ridiculous attempts at hiding from other people. He sees everything and He loves me just the same. He who knew no sin, became sin for us so that we might be made the righteousness of God in Him. 2 Corinthians 5:21 Does that mean I am free to do what I want when I want? No, it means I choose to be obedient because I am restored to God's perfection. I choose God's will, not my own. I consider my life worth nothing to me, if only I may finish the race and complete the task Lord Jesus has given me – the task of testifying to the gospel of God's grace. Acts 20:24 Daughter, your faith has healed you. Go in peace and be freed from your suffering. Mark 5:34

*Dear God,*
*You have established the importance of commitment and covenants.*
*You have witnessed the devastating effects of broken commitments through the ages. Please help to keep my promises and take my commitments seriously. Help me to never commit a sin that passes consequences down to the generations to come. Help me to accept your discipline, be obedient to your word and your law, and to humbly accept the consequences my actions have caused in this life. Those whom You love, you rebuke and discipline.*
*Amen.*

"But where sin increased, grace increased all the more, so that, just as sin reigned in death, so also grace might reign through righteousness to bring eternal life through Jesus Christ our Lord." Romans 5:20-21

-Janet

## Story Eighteen: Joy through God's Provision

I never felt as close to God as I did going through my divorce, which is a miracle considering it came so unexpectedly that it nearly blindsided me. I was pregnant with our second baby when I heard the devastating news that my husband was seeing someone else. This began the long road of healing that would bring me straight to my knees.

After the baby was born, there would be times when my then-husband would come pick up the girls and I would sob in my guest bedroom because that's where I had been sleeping. Then started the cycle--he would pick the girls up, we'd have an argument, and I would come back into the house defeated.

Falling to my knees, I cried out to God: "Why would you let me go through this?"

In September 2023 I heard God speak to me one morning when I was getting ready: "I am going to provide."

But I couldn't picture it.

"Lord, I don't have a job--how am I going to financially make it?" I was stressed about finding a house, stressed about trying to come up with a down payment, stressed about trying to pay my attorney, and yet he said, "I am going to provide."

Today, I can see how far I have already come. Sure, we are living paycheck to paycheck. It's still tough and things are tight. I feel like I cannot get ahead financially and yet, he gave me all I need. I am coming to realize that I try to live too much in the future sometimes instead of taking one day at a time. For example, I have plans to go to PA school-- it's a lot of hard work, but it will be a true blessing. As a single mom, this is my biggest stressor--going back to school and making sure I can still make ends meet.

Where have I seen the Goodness of God in all this? I have seen it in my ex-husband and his new girlfriend when they got me something for Christmas. I've seen it through the mending of relationships in a miraculous way. God has shown me his goodness even when I was mean and they were mean (because hurt people hurt people) and He somehow helped us to find middle ground. I have even seen the hurt start to be healed.

Meanwhile I am trying to live frugally and also remain grateful because his words to me were true: "I am going to provide." And he has.

-Hannah

## Story Nineteen: I Don't Want to Miss it

I can remember thinking there has got to be more to this life then going to work or school. No matter the situation, I always told the Lord: "I don't want to miss it. Whatever it is you have for me, help me to see what you are doing in me through each situation. Just don't let me miss it." There are two big moments in my life when the goodness of God stood out to me-- when I led my dad's siblings to the Lord, and when I was saved during an accident on the mission field.

I never would have guessed I would lead my dad's siblings to the Lord on separate occasions. He was one of four children, with a sister and two brothers. His mom died when he was just 8 years old. The year was 1948, and when his father left, my dad and his three siblings had to stay with their grandparents. No one was ready to take on four kids so close to the other side of the Great Depression, but my dad and his siblings weren't given a choice. Their mother had passed away, their father left them, and as a result, even as adults, they carried a lot of hurt.

When God told me to go and pray for one of my uncles who was very sick, I did not want to listen. I thought I heard him clearly, and when doubt set in, I started resisting the word. One day, my husband was driving home from an afternoon church service when he called me and suggested that we go pray for my uncle. He had heard the exact same thing! This did not make me want to hurry and go pray because I knew there would be crowds of family members there and so I was avoiding the whole situation. When we finally went, one family member after another left the room and we were miraculously almost totally alone. I believe if I had missed the voice of God in this situation, I may have missed the opportunities that came later to lead his other siblings to the Lord.

My husband John once told me: "The safest place to be is in the will of the Lord." This became so true to me on a recent trip to Honduras. I was standing in the kitchen making a meal, when things took a wrong turn. The green beans were added to a big pot of water, and the stove was turned on. After hitting the ignite button, I realized it did not fire up, so I pushed the ignitor a second time. Suddenly, I flashed back to a time when my brother was just three years old. He went to the bathroom and flushed the commode. The sewer line had filled up with gas. In an instant, it exploded, and my baby brother was ablaze from the waist up. The house literally lifted off the foundation. The doctors said my brother wouldn't live through the night and he'd be deaf and blind. He wasn't deaf, and he didn't even wear cheater glasses until he was almost fifty. It was a miracle.

And here I was, standing at the stove, watching that memory flash before my eyes as I saw a great explosion. The walls did not lift off the foundation, but the stove door flew off and locals heard the rumbling all through the mountain, warning people to get back to the ranch because something terrible had happened. Based on the sounds of the stove exploding, as the rest of the team was headed back to the house, they were expecting to see mass carnage. The pieces of the stove that landed on my feet became a boiling fire, and the blazing pain was immediate.

The woman standing to my left when the stove exploded was a nurse, her full RN mode kicked in, and by the time they got my feet to the shower, she was already on the phone with a doctor on her hospital floor back home. That alone was the goodness of God. Being out of the country during something like this can be uneasy, but God saw it fit to put a registered nurse right beside me right when I needed her. She was able to get "doctor's orders" all the way from the states. The oven door had hit my feet, the green beans had exploded into the air. When the ignitor on the stove did not light the first time, that second push was what led to the explosion. And yet I was going to be okay.

The goal in the moments after this accident was to draw the heat out slowly, adding ice to the water a little at a time. The local doctor came, wrapped my feet, and offered to come back the next day to check on me. When the next day rolled around, I wouldn't need the doctor at all. By the time we left to go home a couple days later, I was able to wear my sandals which was miraculous. One of the sweet members of our team, who was 80 years old, asked if he could hug me before we left.

"I thought we'd see carnage when we got back here," he told me.

The night after the accident I got up during the night and saw a light on in the hallway. When I entered the hall, there was a scorpion right there. It's no wonder my 80-year old friend added:

"I love you. In case you are wondering if the devil is trying to kill you, the scorpion is your second notice."

Even after being back home safely, we will never forget it.

The trip to Honduras taught me something. It really is true that the safest place to be is in the will of God. On separate occasions believing that statement allowed me to lead all of my brother's siblings to the Lord. It also allowed me to be at peace in some pretty scary circumstances. In reality, even in uncertain times, he is just wanting our "yes." You can ask yourself: "Even today, Lord, what does that journey look like?" It doesn't mean you'll be in explosions, it might mean that you're the one who will stand in the gap for your family.

The day I mentioned earlier when I met with my uncle, I remember asking him if I could pray for him and he told me yes.

"Have you ever asked Jesus into your heart?" I continued.

"No."

Do you want to?"

"No."

I share this part of the story so people do not get discouraged. We can't make anyone want to accept Jesus. In fact, my uncle, who was sick at the time, went on to live 15 more years. He did get saved years later and even invited me and John to go to church with him before it was all said and done. Maybe I sowed a seed that first time through my prayer over him, or maybe the Lord allowed me to experience the "No" so I could appreciate the miracle when he did finally turn his heart to Him.

The other stories of leading my dad's siblings to the Lord are unique. In another instance, I was in a hospital room with a critically ill uncle. When the boldness came over me, I asked him if he wanted to know Jesus. "Oh baby, everyone does," he told me.

And just like that, I led him in the sinner's prayer in boldness. When the light appears, the darkness will flee. I never thought in a million years I would lead my family to the

Lord. It severed something in the spirit realm. Remember, we all have a story. This journey is just between you and God. He might tell me to pray for someone. I don't want to miss it. He might ask me to lead my family members to Jesus. I don't want to miss it. He may ask me to go to the nations. I don't want to miss it. Even now, as I go through a great trial filled with pain and unknowns, my heart is still postured at peace. Because even in sickness, even in troubled times, I don't want to miss what he has for me.

    -Earlene

## Story Twenty: Open Arms

Seven years ago I was tiptoeing through my house gathering everything I could in a diaper bag as silently as I could. Quietly I snapped my sleeping baby in a car seat. My heart pounded. I scooped my sleeping toddler from her bed. I gently woke my oldest, six years old, and put a finger to my mouth for her to stay quiet. Crashing could be heard in our home, screaming and cursing bounced against the walls. He had drunk too much, taken too many pills. He wasn't a bad person, I told myself so many times. He would be fine once he slept. My pulse thundered louder as my daughter's small hand grabbed mine. My heart broke because she didn't question this moment as we made our way to the door. This wasn't the first time I had whisked her away in the darkness of night.

I strapped my sweet babies in the car. I started the car and we left the driveway and my heart rate slowed. The panic coursing through my body slowly receded. We were safe.

We were headed to my best friend's house. She would open her home to us without question. It was the middle of the night but that didn't matter. She would help me get cartoons going in the living room and get my babies back to sleep. She would let me vent to her and the next day when I went back to the same home to continue life until the next time, she wouldn't judge me. It would be another 4 years before I would realize I couldn't stay in the endless cycle anymore. Over those years plenty of people gave me advice, plenty prayed, many loved me and my babies. Yet it was the steadfastness of a friend that always offered a port in the storm that ultimately would allow me to continue to have faith in a God I couldn't see. She was a woman who truly embodied the love of Jesus, love without strings, compassion, and understanding for me when I didn't even have it for myself.

Christianity to me isn't about how many scriptures you've memorized, services you've attended, prayers you've said. It's faith and love. Love shown to those we may not understand, who may not deserve it in our minds. It's faith that God will do the work needed. We only need to be still, be open to lending our strength to those around us when they are weak and hurting.

Here is to the women who are being that bestie to a friend you desperately wish would wake up and figure it out. Thank you for your patience, thank you for your love, thank you for the amazing job you're doing being a light to someone in need.

Here is to the women that are desperate and feel stranded in the dark. There is a way out. You can do hard things and I'm so proud of you for hanging on.

-Lisa

*"The Lord will fight for you; you need only to be still." Exodus 14:14*

## Story Twenty One: Joy through Infertility

Infertility, 1 in 6 couples struggle to conceive. Never in a million years did I think that would be me and my husband. 1,015 days of waiting, praying and trusting the Lord with our family. In the midst of the valley I struggled to see any goodness of the Lord. I was so angry. Angry at God, that our bodies weren't doing what he so perfectly designed them to do. Angry at everyone around us who so easily conceived and grew their family on their timeline. Angry that we needed help from multiple doctors and tens of thousands of dollars to conceive and grow our family. But God! On the other side of the valley, man, I see His goodness in every single detail of it. My faith grew in ways I didn't know were possible, my relationship with my husband grew, and I learned that I'm capable of facing my fears head on.

I would never wish infertility on anyone, it's a long, lonely and hard road. God provided in ways that when I stop and think about it four years later, I'm still completely blown away.

After being diagnosed with male factor infertility in the beginning of 2021 we were told our chances of conceiving a biological child was very slim. Our doctor advised us to go home and talk about the possibility of using a donor. We were faced with our only option being IVF to grow our family. We didn't know how we would afford it, and secondly I was beyond terrified of needles. It took months of doctors appointments, multiple tests, and surgeries to help us get to the point of even being able to start the process of IVF. Even though God provided for us financially, it was still terrifying but we were jumping all in. After what felt like a crazy round of IVF, we had one perfect little embryo that was completely genetically ours ready for transfer. In December of 2021 we found out that our IVF embryo transfer was successful and that we were going to have a baby!

    I sit writing this next to my now two year old little girl, while I'm pregnant with our second little IVF miracle. I don't take for granted the blessing and the technology that IVF is. Being able to see my child grow from even the cellular level is so incredible it's difficult to even put into words unless you've seen it yourself. We were blessed with the opportunity to pray for our children from the very second the sperm met the egg. It's also not lost on me that we are one of the lucky ones, not everyone goes through IVF and is blessed with a child.

Proverbs 13:12 says "Hope deferred makes the heart sick, but a longing fulfilled is a tree of life." I pray that if your hope is deferred, rather it be infertility or something else that God brings you to your tree of life as well!

    -Molly

## Story Twenty Two: Marriage in Crisis

One Sunday night we had a visiting preacher from Russell Springs, Ky come to speak. It was a great service but what stuck out to me the most was the way my husband was pressing into that service and almost looked to be in turmoil or what they may call radically touched. It was time to go and he couldn't seem to snap out of it. I loved that God was ministering to him so deep but, I'm only human. Therefore, I was also ready for him to get it together so we could go with everyone else to a restaurant for fellowship like we so often did. I suppose he soon pulled himself together enough to go eat and then we went home to get kids in bed late again and fall into bed exhausted, only to hop back up bright and early to get kids to school. During those revival times, we were literally surviving on the grace of God.

I have never experienced a train wreck in my life quite like the one I experienced in that week. After getting kids to school Joey sat me down and shared with me where his heart and life was heading. His heart was certainly not into being married and I still don't even know why he stayed during those years. The night before, God had got ahold of him and he was ready to walk the walk of a true Godly husband. God had given him a clean slate and he knew he had to be brutally honest with me to get there for a fresh new beginning. I will spare you all the details but, while he was feeling like a new man, I found myself suddenly in a marriage that in my eyes, could not be fixed. That same week we found out that Joey was being laid off from his job. Everything came crashing down around me. All I could hear in my head was, "divorced mother of 5". I was lifeless and could see no way out. My perfect life was over. I took to the bed as much as I could when my kids were at school and faked my way through being ok and happy when they were home. My youngest baby, Jade, was 10 months old. She was such a comfort to me during those uncertain times.

I called out to the Lord and He answered me. We began to council with our pastors Jack and Shirley Carter. I was bitter and I was frozen. We needed a miracle. On top of the marriage crisis, counseling made me realize I had some abuse-ish situations in my teenage years that I didn't deem as being anything. So I began to focus on bettering myself and figured I'd divorce eventually but what was the hurry since I had so much on my plate at that moment in my life. When I count up my blessings, I will always count my Pastor Jack Carter and his wife Shirley. Their words were like healing oil and they literally took our hands and walked us through restoration in our marriage. Even if neither of us deserved it, the Lord used them to show us forgiveness and love. They will always be treasured!

Some girlfriends at church decided to literally drag me to a ladies conference in Elizabethtown, Ky, which had to be the Lord. Amy and Joy picked me up and got me there, two women who were not even close friends, joined together by their love for me while I was in crisis. Karen Wheaton was one of the main speakers and this weekend was life changing to me. All I wanted was a divorce and I wasn't backing down. All I needed was the courage to tell my parents and how in the world does one get an attorney and get this Con artist out of my house. One thing I knew, Karen Wheaton had been divorced and she still had the Lord and she was ministering all over creation. I desperately needed to talk to her.

Service got started and her words were like healing oil over my soul. The presence of the Lord was so strong and I truly felt the Lord speaking into my heart. Over and over I heard, "Love your husband". I can still remember rocking my head back and forth as if saying, "No, I will not". I had endured too much in my life. Too much hurt and my self esteem had its last hit. I was done. Then Karen began to sing, "He'll do it again". I crumbled in the presence of God. I was apprehended and comforted by a really great God. The words of her song wrecked me. I'll put them here so you can relate to where I was at this moment.

> *You may be down and feel like God*
>
> *Has somehow forgotten*
>
> *That you are faced with circumstances*
>
> *You can't get through*
>
> *But now it seems that there's no way out*
>
> *And you're going under*
>
> *God's proven time and time again*
>
> *He'll take care of you*
>
> *And He'll do it again*
>
> *He'll do it again*
>
> *If you'll just take a look*
>
> *At where you are now*
>
> *And where you've been*
>
> *Well hasn't He always come through for you*

*He's the same now as then*

*You may not know how*

*You may not know when*

*But He'll do it again*

The weekend was so good and I stayed focused on what God was trying to do in my heart. When the last service was over, I saw that they were ushering Karen Wheaton out the side door and into her van. I was still so desperate to talk to her. I didn't really know that she had people around her to probably keep people like me from bugging her. Or maybe I didn't care. I went out that door and walked as fast as I could and asked her if I could talk to her. She said, "yes" and so I talked as fast as I could and told her my story. Her eyes were so blue and clear as glass as she looked into mine and said, "At all cost, remain with your husband."

She prayed over me and I knew what God was calling me to and I knew the road would be hard. This overwhelming love for my husband came into my heart and I needed that so bad. That day the words to her song that said "He'll find a way to fix this for you" burned into my spirit and for the first time in my life I realized I had my trust misplaced. I was such a scared and dependent little thing. Whether it was my father to protect me and provide or my husband to love me. I trusted man way too much and certainly in the place of my heavenly Father. That day I surrendered all my trust to the Lord Jesus Christ. I didn't know if my husband was going to be perfect for the rest of his life or if he deserved my love and my life. But, I was assured of this one thing, I could trust the Lord to take care of me and all my troubles. I gave Him my heart again and began to lean my ear heavy on His instructions to be a wife who's Heart was running after the ways of the Lord. I trusted in God alone and that is all He required of me!

Once again He healed my heart and once again The Hand of the Lord was upon me. God himself mended our marriage. It took time and it didn't happen overnight. In the midst of our marriage and financial crisis our Pastor suggested we take a cruise with a group of couples from our church including them. It wasn't probably the wisest financial decision we ever made but, we did have the money and we certainly needed some time away from our 5 children all under the age of 7. In the end it was a blessing and the beginning of the healing we so desperately needed.

-Joanie

## Story Twenty Three: Community of Support

When I was asked about a time in my life that I experienced the goodness of God, it was easy for me to recognize the event that shaped deep gratitude in me because not only was my son's life spared, but the community rallied around us in a way that showed us God's love on display. In 2023 in the late summer, when my 13 year-old son John asked to stay the night with his friend and his little brother, I gladly agreed. He wanted to go fishing and I didn't think twice about telling him he could go. I never dreamed that the next day, my whole world would change. Instead of receiving a phone call telling me it was time to pick John up, I answered the phone to a worried voice saying: "He's not breathing."

In this moment, everything stood still. Though I would not know the details at the time, the voice at the other end of the phone belonged to the boys' mom Biranda. When the details of the day emerged later, we learned that John had a seizure and fell into the pond. The boys, having no idea what happened, tried to keep John's head above the water before realizing they needed to go for help. Dragging him in without drowning themselves was not possible. One of the boys ran up to the house for help. Meagan, my former student, who owned the pond where the boys were fishing, would become a lifesaver just moments later. They had asked if they could catch and release at her pond that day, and she had told them sure. When she got a knock on her door from one of the boys telling her John had drowned. Meagan, a former EMT, rushed to pull my son out of the water onto the bank while one of the other boys dialed 9-11. It was a struggle just to pull him out of the pond, due to the heaviness of his body that had taken in so much water.

While John appeared to be losing color and a distinct shade of blue appeared on his face and body, Meagan began CPR. After six rounds, she cried out to God for help. At that moment, John pushed pond water back into her mouth and a coal-like substance began to drain from his nostril. By the time the fire department arrived, he was breathing and responsive. That alone was a miracle.

Fast forward to the phone call. Everything was a blur after hearing the words that my son was not breathing. I had just dropped my daughter Ellie off at band camp and knew my husband, who was leading a band camp at his own school, might not be able to get to the phone. I called my best friend and John's godmother Melissa instead. We met up and started speeding towards the hospital. Melissa fielded all the phone calls-- to the EMTs, to John's pediatrician, who recommended John be life flighted to Vanderbilt University Medical Center. By the time we made it to the hospital, John had already been admitted to the PICU and placed on a ventilator because his lungs were bleeding.

Melissa had it in her heart to host a prayer vigil for John. I did not realize how big our village was, but 100 people showed up for us that night. There was a Facebook Live that I could watch and my friend Marie videoed it. A moment I will never forget is when she scanned the room. Looking at people who had been there at different times throughout our entire life that took the time to show up that day was unbelievable. His friends were there, our friends were there. His old baseball team was there. His current team was there. John's first daycare teacher who was dealing with cancer herself was there. People that hadn't seen John in so many years since he was a little boy chose to come out and pray for him. The feeling of knowing that people were there and cared was powerful and it taught me something. Females in general may struggle with control issues because we think we can take care of everything-- as moms, as professionals, and as wives. At that moment, I realized this was bigger than me. We were sitting in the hospital room and the notifications just kept coming in for people to bless us with their prayers and even financially.

Another moment that was really big to me and my relationship with God was a song by Tasha Layton "Into the Sea (It's Gonna Be Okay) that felt like it was written for us during our hospital stay. I would take a shower, lay down and try to sleep and repeat that song over and over again. I was afraid to go to sleep because I was afraid if I went to sleep, John wouldn't be there when I woke up. In the days and weeks ahead, he did recover from his accident and his lungs strengthened, but what strengthened even more was my faith. The words to that song ring true:

"My heart is breaking

In a way I never thought it could

My mind is racing

With the question, "Are you still good?"

Can you make something

From the wreckage?

Would you take this heart

And make it whole again?

Though the mountains may be moved into the sea

Though the ground beneath might crumble and give way

I can hear my Father singing over me

"It's gonna be okay, it's gonna be okay"

    Through John's Accident, I learned that we have a community of friends and family who were looking out for us, and ultimately showed us the goodness of God. No matter what comes our way, we can choose to believe that "it's all going to be okay."

    -Mendy

## Story Twenty-Four: Building a Warrior

Trials, we all face trials in life, it is inevitable. The uncertainty of what life may bring and what storms we may face, may leave us with a life we never thought we would endure or encounter. Sometimes altering life and leaving us in a place that was not what you thought would be. I faced the trial of an unfaithful marriage I endured for many years. I can spare you the details, but what is more important to share is what actually was birthed in me in the fire. We often pray for the Lord to step in and remove it because he loves us, wishing the trial would stop, that he would save us from such pain and heartache, but that was not the case.

Through the process I found the Lord, and he strengthened me. The fire continued to burn and many times it only got hotter, but I knew I was not alone. As I would cry out to the Lord, he would meet me right there, holding me and comforting me. Psalms 34:18 tells us "The Lord is close to the broken hearted, and saves those who are crushed in spirit."

The Lord is more concerned about the position of our heart and our personal growth in him, than he is in removing or sweeping away the trial. While enduring the flames, I found myself submitting to the Lord, and he used this time to build a warrior in me, to strengthen me, to define me, to teach me who I am in Christ, to build my identity and to build a prayer life I ever knew would ever exist.

At that time in my life I was a lifelong Catholic, who loved the Lord and honored him, feared him, but did not know I could have a relationship with him. What do we do to build a relationship with someone? We spend time with them. By sitting at the feet of Jesus daily, reading the word, praying without ceasing and choosing to worship, he became my strength, he became my protector, he became my source of power and love. With seeking the Lord daily, he clothed me with his identity, therefore my story didn't define me, but the Lord defined me in my story. I began to put on the image of Christ in the midst of this circumstance, to love as he loves, to give as he gives, forgive the unforgivable as he would do, and love the unlovable with the unconditional love of God.

As my journey with the Lord continued and the fire of my trial became hotter, my life verse became- Galatians 6:9 "Let us not become weary in doing what is good, for at the proper time we will reap a harvest if we do not give up." Holding onto this verse and letting the Lord transform me was more fruitful than ever giving up. Jesus was my fourth man in the fire. There were many moments of wanting to give up, throw in the towel and quit, but each time, the Lord would intervene. He saw a greater purpose in my pain and brought forth a new creation in me and taught me to hold on to the destiny of my family.

Jesus himself forgave the very people who killed him and hung him on the Cross--who am I to do anything less than to forgive as well and begin to learn the unconditional love of God? God's agape love means to love someone despite their actions, to love someone who is unlovable, and to love someone without the expectation of receiving anything in return. As I began to learn this type of love for my husband, God put a new perspective on me. A heavenly mindset, to see a person for their God-given destiny and not for who they are being in the moment. To
see past their actions and speak into their destiny and call out the person they are to become through Christ. I will encourage you, as you begin to see through the eyes of Christ, you begin to see the destiny of that person. When you pray into the destiny of that person, it will keep your heart
alive towards that person.

As the Lord has fashioned his promises into your heart, begin to declare the promises over your family and over your husband. As I mentioned above, often my circumstances did not change. The storm would be raging around me, but just as Peter walked on the water when his eyes were on Jesus, he would walk on water and when his eyes would come off of Jesus he would sink. This is the same for us, with my eyes off of Jesus the storm would engulf me and I would feel as if I was sinking, but in the very same moment if I would put my eyes back on Jesus and begin to declare and decree his promises, a warrior would arise.

The warrior that was being built inside of me would stand in authority and I would no longer be sinking. In that moment nothing shifted except my perspective about my circumstances into partnering with the Lord and speaking the things of heaven. This is the authority we have in Christ.

Even though my reality did not look like what I was speaking out, the Lord said, "Hold onto what is true and what is faithful
and speak my heart over this circumstance." I encountered a love that is capable of loving more than I ever knew, this love grew in a time where I was at my darkest. Learning the love of

Christ and being able to look past the actions of others and see them for their destiny was powerful. God's structure of family and the importance of the father's role is of most importance.

During this time, the Lord showed me to speak heavenly things to my children about their father to keep their heart alive towards him, even though his actions may not have warranted that, in the flesh. I believe this was very important because it kept their heart in the position of love. As the outcome of divorce was forced upon me, one thing I knew was I was not going to let the enemy win in any shape or form. With everything the Lord had shown me through the years, Satan may have thought he had won, but he was wrong. Signing divorce papers, I can only describe that weeping as if I was at the funeral of my husband, submitting myself to the Lord in that moment.

Several other moments of such pain and hurt, I would also find myself weeping, and the Lord would come in behind me and hold me as any father would see his daughter's heart weep before him. At that moment, I said aloud, "You're here at this moment too? So I am going to be okay."

In that, my confidence grew and I knew this was not just about restoring my marriage, it was more about restoring my heart to the Father and responding like Jesus. I had the opportunity to put on the image of Christ in any circumstance and seek first the kingdom of God. Honoring the Lord in my choices, freed me and kept my heart in obedience to Him. In return, there was no place for the enemy to win, no matter the circumstance, no matter the actions of others, no matter how hard the enemy tries to create division, putting on the Love of Christ, the radical love of Jesus, will always win.

1 Corinthians 13: 4-7 tells us, "Love is patient, love is kind. It does not envy, it does not boast, it is not proud. It does not dishonor others, it is not self- seeking, it's not easily angered, it keeps no record of wrongs. Love does not delight in evil but rejoices with the truth. It always protects, always trusts, always hopes, always perseveres."

Going through a divorce that I did not want, did not leave me with empty arms when I chose to turn to Jesus. It left me with perspective, purpose and identity.

-April

## Story Twenty Five: The Sun will Come Out

This past weekend held our long-awaited trip to Magic Kingdom, and it has not been everything we wanted it to be for our five-year old daughter Jane. Thanks to a transportation snafu, we got to the park an hour late. I almost cried just trying to find a bathroom. We went to Tomorrowland Speedway (using our lightning pass) only to have the ride shut down the moment before we stepped in the cars. We pivoted and tried the Monsters Inc. show only to have it canceled. Lots of tears from Jane ensued who had been talking about this trip non-stop.

Finally, we got her on a carousel and bought her some ears, and it started looking up. Fast forward a few more rides later, and things are going more smoothly. That is, until we head to lunch. Because of the rain, there are no tables left. People are lingering at most of the inside tables. We get our food, and have walked around everywhere, making laps like it's Black Friday in the mall parking lot.

I thought about my friend Laura Murphy who, before I left school, said she'd pray for sunshine for us. At that moment I thought "praying for sunshine? What? We'll just take what it gives and roll on." Then I thought, maybe praying about the little things that we can often figure out on our own, is worth doing too.

So standing in the middle of Tomorrowland's Starlight Cafe, I prayed that we'd find a table in the nick of time so we could feed a hangry 5 year old and help her recover from Space Mountain (she was terrified). The fountain drinks were cold in my hands as I scanned the crowded porch area. I hear a woman with a French accent ask if we are looking for seats, motioning us to her table where her family is packing up. Tears welled. Prayer answered.

I think about God being there for us in the big things: my son's death, life changes, big decisions. It's easy to forget that He wants us in the little moments too. And by the way, after lunch, the sun came out, shining brightly as a reminder that the storm will not last forever.

-Jessica

# My STORY

"Weeping may last for the night, but Joy comes in the morning." -Psalms 30:5

"Man makes his plan, but the Lord orders his steps."
-Proverbs 16:9

"Be anxious for nothing, but in everything with prayer and supplication, let your request be made unto God."

"…And the peace of God that supasses all understanding will guard your heart and mind in Christ Jesus." -Philippians 4:6-7

"For I know the plans I have for you," declares the Lord. "Plans to prosper you and not harm you. Plans for hope and a future." Jeremiah 29:11

"God is within her, she will not fall." Psalms 46:5

"Trust in the Lord with all your heart and lean not on your own understanding." -Proverbs 3:5

"She speaks with wisdom and teaches with kindness." She opens her mouth with discretion, and on her tongue is the law of kindness." -Proverbs 31:25

"And we know that in all things God works for the good of those who love him, who have been called according to his purpose." -Romans 8:28

"I praise you because I am fearfully and wonderfully made; your works are wonderful, I know that fully well." Psalms 139:14

"Do not lose heart when doing good, for in due season you will reap a harvest if you do not give up." Galatians 6:9

"The Lord delights in those who fear him, who put their hope in his unfailing love." Psalm 147:11

"For where your treasure is, your heart will be also." Luke 12:34

"Many are the plans in a person's heart, but it is the Lord's purpose that prevails."

"The Lord is with me. I will not be afraid." Psalm 118:6

"But I, with a song of Thanksgiving, will sacrifice to you. What I have vowed, I will make good." -Jonah 2:9

"For God so loved the world that he gave his only son, that whoever believes in Him would not perish, but have everlasting life." - John 3:16

"The fruit of the righteous is a tree of life, and the one who is wise saves lives." Proverbs 11:30

"May the God of hope fill you with all joy and peace in believing." -Romans 15:13

"Count it all joy, my brothers, when you meet trials of various kinds." James 1:2

"But the fruit of the spirit is love, joy, peace, patience, kindness, goodness, faithfulness." Galatians 5:22

"A joyful heart is good medicine…" Proverbs 17:22

"The hope of the righteous brings joy, but the expectation of the wicked will perish." -Proverbs 10:28

"But those who wait on the Lord will renew their strength; They shall mount up with wings like eagles, They shall run and not be weary." Isaiah 40:31

"I sought the Lord and He answered me and delivered me from all my fears." Psalm 34:4

"Come to me all you who are weary and burdened, and I will give you rest." Matthew 11:28

Final Story: Words of Wisdom

    God wants us to fully embrace and enjoy the gift of this life. Thankfully, though, this life is not the end. We are part of a purpose that is greater than a mere lifespan. There may be situations we have wept and prayed over. When we realize we are eternal beings, and life itself continues on unending, then it is not so discouraging to accept that the answers may fully manifest beyond our current lifespan.

    We have hope in the God of hope, who hears every heart cry and sees every tear that falls. We shall know joy in the presence of the One who promises to wipe away all tears from our eyes. An eternal perspective changes everything. Now is important for us, and to God. But the ever-present God is not limited to 70-80 years. He is present in all of eternity. And, in Him, we are not limited, either. Nothing has been in vain. We are part of something much bigger than what we can discern with our physical senses.

-Cheryl Spencer
11/21/21

Special thanks to:

Andrea King, Tammy Thompson, Faith Harralson, Gaye Rogers, Ashley Proctor, Melissa Bullington, Hannah Thornton, Shirl Nafziger-Lyne, Jodie Bivens, Natalie Tanner, Elisha Lyne, Ashley Roberts, Katie Aud, Trish Clark, Krislyn Brown, Brooke Parker, Janet Rowland, Hannah Blandford, Earlene Docimo, Lisa Grigsby, Molly Hagan, Joanie Hagan, Mendy Rue, April Peech, Jessica Jones, Hannah Thornton, and Cheryl Spencer for letting your story be heard. Your "yes" to share a piece of the goodness of God stirs up faith in everyone who reads it.

A special thanks also goes to my mom, Cheryl Spencer who had the dream of becoming a published author. Now her words, forever in print in this journal, are a reminder that there is power in sharing our hearts with others, for the words we share will outlive our physical time on earth. I love that you instilled in Lisa and me a love for words, from the first Dr. Suess books we read as little children to the journals we sift through today as we cling to nuggets of wisdom you left behind.

I also want to thank Earlene Docimo, who became a spiritual mom to me, for standing in the place of my mom as I navigated my first years without her. From helping me move into my new home to financially supporting us in unexpected ways, to offering me Godly wisdom and counsel, I love you tremendously and honor the way you taught me to say: "I don't want to miss it."

Made in the USA
Monee, IL
10 February 2025